# The Situation

Adriana Locke

UMBRELLA
PUBLISHING INC.

This is a work of fiction. Names, characters, organizations, places, events, and incidents are either products of the author's imagination or are used fictitiously. Otherwise, any resemblance to actual persons, living or dead, is purely coincidental.

Copyright © 2025 by Adriana Locke
All rights reserved.

No part of this book may be reproduced, or stored in a retrieval system, or transmitted in any form or by any means, electronic, mechanical, photocopying, recording, or otherwise, without express written permission of the publisher.

Published by Umbrella Publishing, Inc.

Special Edition Paperback ISBN: 978-1-960355-35-5

**NO AI TRAINING:** Without in any way limiting the author's [and publisher's] exclusive rights under copyright, any use of this publication to "train" generative artificial intelligence (AI) technologies to generate text is expressly prohibited. The author reserves all rights to license uses of this work for generative AI training and development of machine learning language models.

Cover Design by Kari March
Cover Photography by Michelle Lancaster @lanefotograf
Special Edition Cover Design by Books and Moods

# Books by Adriana Locke

*My Amazon Store*

*Signed Copies*

*Brewer Family Series*

The Proposal | The Arrangement | The Invitation | The Merger | The Situation

*Carmichael Family Series*

Flirt | Fling | Fluke | Flaunt | Flame

*Landry Family Series*

Sway | Swing | Switch | Swear | Swink | Sweet

*Landry Family Security Series*

Pulse

*Gibson Boys Series*

Crank | Craft | Cross | Crave | Crazy

*The Mason Family Series*

Restraint | The Relationship Pact | Reputation | Reckless | Relentless | Resolution

*The Marshall Family Series*

More Than I Could | This Much Is True

*The Exception Series*

The Exception | The Perception

*Dogwood Lane Series*
**Tumble | Tangle | Trouble**

*Standalone Novels*
**Sacrifice | Wherever It Leads | Written in the Scars | Lucky Number Eleven | Like You Love Me | The Sweet Spot | Nothing But It All | Between Now and Forever**

For a complete reading order and more information, visit www.adrianalocke.com.

# Synopsis

Someone should tell Tate Brewer that one-night stands aren't supposed to come with a sequel.

I've learned the hard way—don't be reckless with anything, least of all my heart. But after one too many vodka sodas, saying yes to a much younger, devastatingly smooth stranger for one wild night seems like the perfect way to forget my brutal divorce. I even gave him a fake name. What could go wrong?

*You'd be surprised.*

Because instead of being my spicy little secret, Tate is now the chief marketing officer at my new job. He's determined to prove our night together was only the beginning—and he has the tools to do it.

Chiseled jaw. Washboard abs. Effortless charm. He's as sinful as he is sweet and knows exactly how to get under my skin and melt my defenses.

I wanted a one-night stand. Instead, I got a "situation."

# Cast of Characters

*parents*

    **Rory Brewer** - matriarch of the family; divorced and dating again

    **Reid Brewer** - patriarch of the family; divorced and in prison

*siblings*

    **Gannon Brewer** [*The Merger*] - the oldest Brewer sibling; president of Brewer Group

    **Jason Brewer** [*The Arrangement*] - CEO of Brewer Air; former military/private security

    **Renn Brewer** [*The Proposal*] - retired rugby player

    **Ripley Brewer** [*The Invitation*] - exercise physiologist

    **Bianca Brewer** [*Flame*] - former Interim President of Brewer Group; moved to Florida and got married

    **Tate Brewer** [*The Situation*] - Director of Operations at Brewer Group

## Chapter One

# Aurora

"I'm doing it." The strap of my bag bites into my shoulder as I step forward. "By the time I'm back in this airport tomorrow night, it'll be done."

The airline check-in officer lifts a brow, pinning me to the spot with the scrutiny of someone paid to catch people doing inconspicuous things in airports.

"Oh no. It's not like that," I say hurriedly, gesturing to my earbuds. "I'm talking to a friend."

Jamie's snort pierces my eardrums. "*Lying to a friend* is more like it."

"I'm a model citizen," I say, ignoring her. "You don't have to worry about me. I'm harmless."

"Only criminals say that," Jamie says.

I fight the urge to roll my eyes, not wanting the officer to think I'm getting snarky with her. The last thing I need is to get apprehended by the marshals and miss my flight. That would be a great way to start the weekend.

The agent doesn't respond. Instead, she dismisses me with a flick of her gaze toward the jetway.

"Thank you. Have a great day." I scurry to catch up with the other people waiting to board the flight.

Raindrops splatter against the tunnel, carried by a howling wind that began minutes ago. The jetway trembles from the onslaught, and the other passengers exchange worried glances. I chew on my bottom lip in frustration. *This flight better not get delayed.*

"What is that sound?" Jamie asks as my line begins to move.

"The wind. Is it storming at the salon?"

"No, although it looks like it could start at any moment. Maybe it'll knock the power out, and I'll have to cancel this afternoon's appointments. Maddie Spriggs is supposed to be here in an hour. I'd be beside myself if I had to postpone her cut and color."

I laugh and step onto the plane. "Sure, you would."

"Welcome aboard," a smiling flight attendant says.

I nod, grip my bag tightly, and fight the urge to ask if she's concerned about potential delays. Slowly, the bodies in front of me find their seats, and I reach mine—seat 4A.

*First class and a window seat? Score!*

"At least if I die, I'll know what first class feels like." I sink into the roomy blue pleather. "You should see how wide these seats are. I can put my arms down and not elbow whoever sits next to me."

"Don't talk about dying," Jamie says. "What am I supposed to do if you die?"

I plop my bag at my feet and appreciate the extra space. "Oh, sure. Make my theoretical death about you."

"Who else would it be about? I'd be here to deal with the salon *and* your customers, who would naturally be devastated. They'd expect me to console them, but—I don't know whether you know this about me—I'm not the consoling kind."

*The Situation*

I laugh again, imagining my best friend trying to handle other people's emotions. It would not end well.

Jamie Ralston is known for many things. She's one of the best hairstylists in Nashville and owns one of the most popular salons, The Luxe. Her sense of humor is unmatched. She has an unbelievable shoe collection, knows every lyric to every country song written in the past thirty years, and has perfected the pouty red lip. But she's the last person I'd go to for emotional support unless I'm ready to hear the raw, ugly truth.

"How long is your flight?" she asks.

"It's just over an hour. I brought my earbuds and a book. I can't think of the last time I got to sit quietly on a plane and read."

"After the past year and a half, that's the least you deserve."

*I couldn't agree more.*

The past eighteen months have been nothing short of brutal. My ex-husband, Kent, made it his mission to make my life a living hell. Although he took a job in Japan and moved across the world, he fought me tooth and nail *over everything*. The house. The car. Our frequent flier miles and bank accounts were a biggie. But the bastard even fought me over the damn blender our friends gave us as a housewarming gift and the jewelry box I bought on our honeymoon.

"I miss you around here," Jamie says. "The Luxe isn't the same without you."

"I'll be back in town tomorrow night."

"You know what I mean." She huffs. "I know your new job is what you wanted, *and I'm so happy for you.*" The way she says it, as if a gun is pointed at her head, makes me laugh. "I haven't even tried to fill your chair. I don't want to think about working alongside someone else."

"If I hate this new gig, I'll return to the salon full-time. You know that."

"And we both know you won't. You're going to be so damn good that they'll promote you within a week, and you'll be running the damn place."

"I love how supportive you are about this. Did you get that whole thing out without rolling your eyes?"

"No. They're still rolling."

I laugh, digging around my bag for my book, and then I slide my purse under the seat in front of me.

The cabin air is thick and balmy, thanks to the rain pelting the windows. The sky is less angry than before I boarded and not quite as dark, but the buckets of precipitation haven't waned. I slip my sweater off my shoulders before I sit back again.

"It's so humid in here," I say, gathering my dark hair at the nape of my neck. "If this plane gets delayed, I'm going to be pissed."

"The weatherman just said the storm is passing quickly, so you should be clear."

"Good."

"So you get into Columbus this evening. Then what? Do you go straight into the event activities?"

I fashion my locks into a low-hanging knot to keep my hair off my neck. "I don't have anything until tomorrow. The original plan was to leave here tomorrow morning, but if I did that, I'd be scrambling as soon as I landed. That left me with this flight or one that leaves at ten o'clock tonight, and I hate landing in a new city and getting to the hotel when it's dark outside."

"That's fair. So you'll hang out tonight? Order some room service?" She pauses. *"Go on the prowl?"*

My laugh is quicker and louder than I intended, and I capture a few curious looks from passengers lining the aisle.

"I'm serious," Jamie says. "You've been separated for almost two freaking years, and now you're officially divorced from the asshole. You need to get back out there before you forget how."

"Trust me. I won't forget how. It's practically all I think about sometimes."

*Lately? Most of the time.*

I haven't been with anyone since Kent. When our marriage fell apart, it took my sex drive with it. The idea of being with a man was wholly uninspiring for the longest time, and fighting over lawn mowers and quilts for months on end is just short of getting doused with a bucket of iced water on repeat.

But a month ago, I picked up my first romance novel in years. My sex drive is suddenly back and very, *very* needy.

"Then what's stopping you?" she asks. "You keep telling me you're too busy—blah, blah, blah. One of these days, you'll have to take the leap and dive back in."

"I've been divorced for three weeks, Jamie. It's not like I'm avoiding it."

"It looks like you're avoiding it to me. It doesn't take that much time to have a one-night stand."

I roll my eyes, fumbling with the tray table. *How in the heck does this thing come out?* "I'm just getting to know myself for the first time. A preacher raised me, remember? I've spent most of my life in a relationship or feeling guilty for lusting after men I wasn't married to." The tray table frees from the armrest. *Presto!* "I'm just not sure what I want, and I don't want to make mistakes this time."

"I'll tell you what didn't look like a mistake—and that was the Daddy in the salon the other day," she says.

"More like Granddaddy." I laugh. "Besides, that man had red flags the size of Texas."

"That might be true. We all know I can't see red regarding warning signs in men."

"*That* is definitely true," I say, reminded of the litany of men who Jamie should've steered away from and ran toward instead.

"What about the hot cowboy you told me about from the grocery store?" she asks. "Anything on that front?"

"No."

"Ror—"

"He wasn't my type!"

She groans. "Hot cowboys are everyone's type."

"Not true. *Darlin'* is cute once or twice. He would've been much hotter if he had stopped talking."

"Do you know what your problem is?" she asks. "It's that you don't appreciate God's gifts. You're a beautiful woman with a body I'd do anything but run for, and a personality that's good enough to make you my best friend, and you don't appreciate any of it."

My giggle turns into a full-out laugh.

"What do you want?" she asks. "What are we looking for? A professional? A man riding a motorcycle who's running from the law? Or do you want a sexy co-ed fresh out of a history lecture? The opportunities are endless, my friend."

"I don't want anyone too young. I don't want to be their mommy." I notice the woman sitting across the aisle side-eyeing me, so I twist away from her in my seat and lower my voice again. "I'm 100 percent sure I'm going to be on some kind of watch list after today."

I glance up as the flight attendant pauses beside me.

"Can I get you something to drink before we take off?" she asks.

"*Oh.*" *That's a thing?* "Water would be nice. Thank you."

She nods and turns to Ms. Eavesdropper.

"I can get used to first class," I say. "You get wide seats *and* drinks before takeoff. Can it get any better?"

"In my next life, I'm getting a fancy job that wants to fly me to events first class and pay for hotel suites."

"Let's hope it continues to be amazing. I've only worked here for two months. There's still time for it to go to shit."

"You say that from your comfy seat in the front of the plane." She sighs dramatically. "I'm going to call my mom and tell her she was wrong. Cheerleading could've paid off for me big time. I mean, all that math and science crap didn't get me anywhere. I do hair for a living."

"You're doing just fine for yourself, Miss Salon of the Year for six straight years."

"Yeah, but I could be flying to Columbus, drinking champagne, and wearing cute clothes while schmoozing on someone else's dime."

"Well, when you put it like that …"

*The Situation*

"Face it. I'm never wrong." She yawns. "I gotta go. Maddie will arrive soon, and I must mentally prepare for her drama."

"Have fun."

"*You have fun*. Be safe. Drink your water. And call me when you land."

"Yes, Mom."

She laughs. "Love you, Ror."

"Love you. Bye."

"Bye."

I end the call and pull out my earbuds.

The sky is much brighter, and the rain is more of a mist than a shower. Steam rises from the tarmac below.

A spark of excitement flickers inside me. I sit with it, holding my book on my lap, and enjoy the peace in my body. Finally, I can breathe without wincing. I can hope without it feeling pointless. I'm able to look toward *my* future and dream about the possibilities.

I'm free to … *be me*.

"Here's your water, ma'am," the flight attendant says.

I turn to take my drink from her, but instead of reaching for it, my attention focuses on a man standing at the front of the plane.

Ocean-colored eyes. Square jawline. *Sinful smirk*.

Whoever is on the other end of his call must be getting an earful because the veins in his temple pulse.

"Thank you," I say, taking my drink from the flight attendant.

She glances over her shoulder, then grins at me knowingly.

The man passes aisle one and then aisle two. The lady by the window nearly breaks her neck looking at him. Aisle three is full. Chaos floods my body as he gets closer.

He stops at the seat next to me, flashing a killer smile my way.

*Jamie, I'm sorry I lied to you.*

I return his smile.

*First class could—and did—get a whole lot better.*

## Chapter Two

### Aurora

*Take a breath.*

"Hey," he says, his tone entirely too sexy for a random Friday afternoon on an airplane.

"Hey."

His mischievous grin tugs at the corners of my mouth as I smile wider.

He sits, sliding his bag onto the floor. It gives me a moment to take him in—and get myself together.

A white shirt loosely hugs his torso, giving a delicious hint of the hard pecs and washboard abs that I'm sure lie beneath it. One wrist is adorned with a heavy-looking watch, and his waist is wrapped with a brown leather belt. It ties into the golden-brown blazer, highlighting his broad shoulders.

His warm, creamy cologne kisses the air as he settles into his

*The Situation*

seat. He sits with his knees slightly apart, and they almost touch mine. His fingers slide down his thick thighs clad in dark navy pants. I hold myself back from letting my leg "accidentally" bump his to feel the spark I'm sure would race through my blood from the contact.

"This is the moment when I say something clever and you laugh," he says, his gaze dancing with amusement. "But I have completely lost my train of thought."

"Why?"

"Because I expected to sit next to someone much older *and much less attractive* than you."

"*Oh okay*," I say, my cheeks growing warm. "That's smooth."

"I'm glad I haven't lost my touch." He lets his smile linger for a long moment, and its heat curls through my veins. "I'm Tate."

*And I'm screwed—and not in the way I'd like to be right now.*

"I'm Kelly," I say, uninterested in giving this twentysomething hottie my real name—just in case. Red flags aren't always apparent in the first two minutes. Besides, so far, he seems too good to be true. "Kelly Kapowski."

"Kelly Kapowski, it's a pleasure to meet you."

The pilot's voice comes through the overhead speakers, interrupting our exchange. Tate watches me expectantly, as if he thinks I'll be eager to reengage with him as soon as the takeoff instructions have been delivered. While I'm not adverse to flirting with a handsome stranger, I am uninterested in sitting beside him and frothing at the mouth.

Been there, done that, and have two divorces to prove it.

I open my book and find where I left off this morning, pointedly ignoring my seatmate. But no matter how many times I re-read the first line of the chapter, I can't forget Tate is beside me. I can't let the story overtake him. Every tap of his foot and wiggle of his fingers stokes a fire in my belly—one I'm desperate to ignore.

He clears his throat, but I don't look up. I can feel his gaze on my face, almost as if he's willing me to lift my chin. The longer I don't make eye contact or give him attention, the more he shifts in his seat like the silence is killing him.

"What are you reading?" he asks once we're at cruising altitude.

"A book," I say without looking up.

"What kind of a book? Thriller? Biography? Nonfiction?"

"It's a romance novel."

"What's it about? And don't say romance."

I hide a smile and finally raise my gaze to his, only to catch his eyes sparkling. *Good God.*

"It's about what every romance novel is about—a happy ending," I say.

Seconds go by as my words sink into his brain. His brows lift, and a slow, sexy smile slips across his lips.

"Is that an innuendo?" he asks.

"Maybe."

"Now I'm curious." He glances at the book cover. "What's the plot? Or is it just ... *happy endings?*"

"There are enough of both to be satisfying."

I lift my book and try to focus on the first line once again. But I don't get past the fifth word before he speaks.

"What are you doing?" he asks, sliding his large hands down his thighs.

*Is he serious?* "Reading."

"What am I supposed to do if you're reading?"

*Oh my God.* I sigh and look at him. "I don't know. Didn't you bring a book or work or something?"

"Sure. But I'd rather talk to you." He smiles broadly, as if this angle of attack usually works. "So are you going home to Columbus or visiting?"

I contemplate not answering him and sticking my nose back in my book. But he will poke at me until I cave ... and I *will* cave. Being flirted with by him is a bit of an ego boost, whether he's seriously flirting with me or not.

"I'm going for work," I say, closing my novel.

*The Situation*

He folds his hands on his lap, looking far too pleased with himself. *Cheeky fucker.*

"Same," he says. "What do you do for work?"

"I just started a new job. We're crafting a new marketing position, so there isn't an official title yet. What about you?"

"On paper, I'm the director of operations for an investment firm. But I'm really the guy who cleans up messes my boss isn't good enough to fix."

"There are worse things you could do for a paycheck. At least he sends you first class, right?"

"I suppose that's true," he says, smiling as if there's a joke I don't understand. "He's just a prick and sends me everywhere he doesn't want to go himself."

"No offense, but I think that's just what bosses do."

"Whose side are you on, Kelly Kapowski?"

I fight a giggle at the name and his obliviousness to it. "I'm not on anyone's side. I'm just the casual, neutral observer. But if he's such a prick, have you considered looking for another job?"

"I can't. It's complicated."

*What's that supposed to mean?* "What about asking him for a transfer? Tell him you feel stagnant, and your creative juices could be used better in a new position. Anyone in management should appreciate your honesty. Besides, you perform best when doing something you want to do."

His eyes sweep the length of my body. "You're right. When I do what I want, my performance is unbeatable."

*Oh my God.* My heart flutters wildly as I absorb the heat in his gaze. That line has several solid comebacks, but for the life of me, I can't think of one.

"On a serious note," he says, "if I tell anyone I can use my *creative juices in a new position*, it won't be my boss."

I laugh. "Okay, maybe you shouldn't use that phrase at all. *Juices* aren't very sexy."

"That's a matter of opinion."

"I'd challenge you to use *juices* in a sentence and make it sexy, but now probably isn't the right time." I glance up at the flight attendant, waiting for our drink order. "Another water for me, please."

"Me, too. Thank you." Tate throws her for a loop with his smile before returning to me. "I'll take up that challenge when we have more privacy. But, for now, back to romance novels. Do you always read them, or is this a one-off?"

"A one-off?" I gasp in faux horror. "I'm firmly in my romance era, thank you very much."

"Aren't women always in their romance era?"

"All of the ones who want a happy ending," I say with a wink.

"There are places besides romance novels to get those, you know."

"Yes, and half of the places that advertise them lie."

He lifts a brow and smirks. "There are still half who deliver beyond expectations."

"And they always believe their product is the best on the market, so it costs too much to be worth the risk."

He leans toward me, his eyes shifting from blue to green so wildly that it's impossible to look away. "I happen to know of a happy ending free trial going on this weekend."

I burst out laughing, pulling away from him.

I take my new drink from the flight attendant and hand her my original water glass, making a concerted effort not to touch Tate.

Although I'm sure he's just playing with me, this back-and-forth is just what I need. I haven't admitted it to Jamie or anyone, for that matter, but I've been a little scared about the whole dating thing. It's been so long since I've done it, and my experience is so little to begin with. It's only been a few weeks since the official end of my marriage, and I've felt a little frozen.

*But this conversation with Tate?* The ice is melting away.

"I didn't see a wedding ring," he says. "Does that mean there's no Mr. Kapowski?"

I laugh. "Is that your slick way of asking if I'm married?"

He takes a drink, watching me over the rim. "I just want to know if I have any competition."

"Competition? For what?"

"For you."

*This charming bastard.* "You are so full of shit."

"Am I?"

I take a long drink, giving my heart a chance to stop pounding against my ribs.

"Think about it," he says. "You're in your romance era. I'm in my bored era. We're both just people looking for happy endings."

"Your *bored era*?" I snort-laugh. "What the hell does that mean?"

"It means I'm bored. Dating has lost its luster. It's the same routine over and over, and I'm tired of it. I'm ready for something real."

My heart swells at his response even though I'm not entirely convinced it's an honest answer. Maybe I'm cynical, but it's hard to believe that a man like him wants to settle down. He's gorgeous, young, and undoubtedly has his pick of women. He can't make me believe he's looking to settle down. I call bullshit.

I narrow my eyes skeptically.

"My friends are all married and having kids," he says. "I'm quickly becoming the fun uncle who shows up on birthdays and holidays with loud, messy presents."

I laugh. "I feel your pain on that one. My friends are having children now, and I'm the fun auntie."

"Do you want kids?"

*Do I want kids?* Startled, I take another drink. That question is very personal and not fully straightforward. I'm not willing to discuss it with a random man on a plane.

"I'll just say that I spent more time at home working on my cozy-girl persona than I do trying to pick up a man to make babies with," I say.

"Like you have a hard time picking up men. Come on."

I pull my sweater onto my shoulders before snuggling into the seat. "Picking up a man and picking up a man I'd have children with are two very different things."

He nods as he processes that. "Fair. Now, what's a cozy-girl persona?"

"Why are you asking so many questions?"

"How else do I get to know you?"

"You don't."

"Why not?"

I laugh, amused. "Because it doesn't matter. We're going to land in a bit, and you'll never see me again, so why bother trying to get to know the nuts and bolts of my life?"

"Women typically love to tell me all about themselves," he says curiously. "I'm not sure what the problem is here."

I lean against the console separating us, holding his gaze. "I'm going to go out on a limb here and say that most of the women you're referring to are about your age."

He shrugs noncommittally.

"And that would be the problem," I say.

"I don't understand."

I smile. "The women you typically engage with are at one stage of life, and I am at another. They're in their twenties and have energy to toss around. On the other hand, I'm just looking forward to getting to my hotel and having dinner at this cute little restaurant called Ruma inside the hotel, if I can get in, before going to my room, lighting a candle, and taking a hot bath." I shrug. "We aren't the same."

"But you still want to have dinner with me tonight, right?"

I laugh, sitting back again as the pilot's voice crackles through the speakers. He welcomes us to Columbus and gives us the time and temperature. The flight attendant walks by, ensuring we're buckled, and takes our drinks and napkins.

"You didn't answer me," he says.

My stomach swirls, and I make a concerted effort to breathe

*The Situation*

smoothly. His question—so direct and pointed—catches me off guard. *Does he really want to see me tonight?*

He watches me closely, making it clear that he's dead serious. There's no laugh, no smirk. He doesn't flinch. He simply waits for my response.

I shift in my seat as my mind races. His offer is a nice boost to my confidence, which I appreciate. But as I notice every woman in our vicinity keeps stealing glances at him and soak in just how handsome he is, reality settles in.

Nothing good can come out of this.

At best, I see him for dinner. At worst, I give him my number, and he never calls. Either way, I don't want to be in my hotel room tonight wondering if the phone will ring.

It took me eighteen months to end that kind of situation the last time, and I have no interest in repeating it anytime soon—or ever. Besides, this weekend is about work. I need to focus on that.

"I don't typically set up dinner dates with men I've only just met on planes," I say. "Sorry."

"What are the requirements then?"

*Huh?* "What do you mean?"

"Tell me what I need to do to see you tonight."

His features change, morphing into the serious businessman who boarded the plane. The glimmer in his eyes is intense. The lines on his forehead pull together as if he's closing a deal. Only ... *I'm* the deal this time.

The plane descends from the sky and lands smoothly onto the runway. I grip the armrests and hold tight until we come to a crawl. The roar of the engines blocks any opportunity to chat, and I'm grateful for that. It'll end the conversation organically.

The plane comes to a standstill, and the lights flicker on. Passengers stand and gather their things. *But Tate?* He remains sitting and facing me.

"I really want to see you again, Kelly."

My stomach flutters. His determination is sexy, and being the object of his attention is heady. If this were another time and place ... But it's not.

I drag my eyes across his stubbled jaw, over those kissable lips, and along the length of his body.

"I don't have time," I say although that's not entirely true. "I have dinner plans tonight, work all day tomorrow, and then I'm back on a flight home. Thank you, though. You're good for my ego."

He holds my gaze for a long moment. Then he stands and lifts his bag off the floor before turning to me. "Until we meet again, Miss Kapowski."

He flashes me one final cocky smile that I feel in my core before disappearing into the throng of people shuffling off the plane. I watch him as he goes, both elated at the attention and frustrated all the same.

Turning down what might be the hottest man I've ever seen in the flesh while living in a state of sexual deprivation deserves a gold medal.

*"I really want to see you again, Kelly."*

I giggle, shoving my book in my bag.

*At least I still got it. Or, at least, Kelly does.*

## Chapter Three

# Tate

I close my computer and pick up my ringing phone, glancing at the screen before I say hello.

"Hey, Gannon," I say, standing.

"I just returned to the office from a meeting with McCabe."

I snort, stretching my arms overhead.

"Don't start your shit," Gannon says.

"Then don't start a conversation by painting a picture of you in a hockey facility. I can't help that's fucking hilarious."

"You are so easily amused."

I chuckle and move to the windows overlooking the city. Although I won't admit it openly to him, Gannon is right. When it comes to this issue, it's time to be serious.

The Tennessee Raptors hockey team is the biggest thorn in my family's professional side. It was Dad's baby. Despite adding to the Brewer portfolio, taking on other projects and teams, *and having kids,* the Raptors were his greatest love. Naturally, when he went to prison a few years ago, and we had to sort through the mess he left behind, the Raptors were a full-blown disaster. None of us wanted to take it on, so we left it for last.

"McCabe gave me his two weeks' notice," Gannon says, dropping the news onto my lap like a barbell.

"What? You're kidding me."

"Unfortunately, I'm not."

"Why?" I ask.

"Someone in his family, maybe a parent, is sick, possibly with cancer."

I shake my head, admiring my abs in the reflection. *This would make a good selfie.* "How do you not pay attention when someone shares such personal news with you?"

"Because I don't care what's happening in his personal life." He sighs. "But I do care that the Raptors are without a marketing director. Again."

"How far was McCabe on the rebrand?"

"The last full update was two weeks ago. He has a great plan and a hundred balls in the air, but I don't know who will catch them now. I'd just as soon sell the team instead of dealing with it. But no one will buy it for a reasonable price in this state."

I gaze across the city and mull over the situation. It would take a lot of stress off Gannon's plate as the president of Brewer Group, the umbrella company that owns the Raptors, to have it sorted. I want that for him. He deserves to be able to go home at night to his fantastic wife and beautiful baby girl.

We all deserve to put this last piece of Dad's legacy to bed. Once and for all.

But the hockey team needs a thorough refresh—spun in a complete one-eighty. It has to be completely detached from its current reputation with a new logo, mascot, and a *whole new vibe.* We have to make it an active participant in the community instead of a talking point whenever the word *scandal* is brought up in conversation.

"I don't need this headache," Gannon groans. "Help me out. Do you have any suggestions? We can't just hire someone off the street, and I exhausted my contact list when I hired McCabe. Ripley gave me one name. Renn had nothing. Jason is useless in sports, and Bianca sent a shrugging emoji when I asked her."

"Oh, so I'm your last call?"

"Don't take it personally."

"I take everything personally. How could it not be personal? Think about it—if you call me first or last, it's a silent display of where I rank in your mind. Did you think of me first, or Jason? That shows how much faith you have in me."

"Stop with the baby of the family bullshit *and help me.*"

I sigh for his benefit. "I wouldn't be so mean to someone I needed —especially if they were my last resort—but whatever."

Gannon doesn't say a word. He doesn't make a sound. Somehow, his irritated silence is louder than anything.

*"Fine,"* I say. "I don't happen to have any names handy, but let me talk to some people at the event tomorrow night and see what shakes out."

"Do you know what I really need? I need a brother who likes hockey."

"What? *No.* No, no, no. Don't even put that into the universe, asshole. With our dad, we could have a brother come out of the woodwork at any point. And, with our luck, he'd be a chip off the old block."

A knock comes from the hallway.

"Hang on a second," I say.

I grab several bills from my wallet. Then I pull open the door and find an older man in a suit and tie holding a single long-stemmed red rose.

"Good evening, sir," he says, handing me the flower.

"Good evening." I slip the cash into his palm. "Thank you for your help. I appreciate you."

"Anytime, sir. Thank you. Have a wonderful evening."

*That's the plan.*

He flashes me a smile and then scoots toward the elevator.

I let the door swing shut behind me.

The energy I've been fighting to keep under control all afternoon and evening surges forward, filling every cell in my body. Kelly's grin tugs at my heart. The curve of her shoulder as it gently slopes to her neck knots my stomach. *The way she turned me down?* It fucks with me.

Hard.

"Who was that?" Gannon asks.

"I had something brought to my room," I say, unable to fight the smile slipping across my lips.

"Where are you this weekend, anyway?"

I place the flower on the desk, then head into the bedroom.

"That's rude," I say.

"What? Why is that rude?"

"You order me to these random places to do your bidding against my will, then you act like it's so unimportant that you don't even need to remember where you sent me." I shake my head. "If it's not important, for the love of God, Gannon—let me stop traveling so damn much."

He groans. "Not this again, Tate. I don't have time to listen to you whine right now."

*Fucker.*

"You're lucky because I don't have time to whine right now," I say, standing in the middle of the bedroom. *What time should I head downstairs?* "Although, make no mistake, I will complain to everyone who will listen once I'm back in the office on Monday. Because it's complete bullshit that our family-owned airline couldn't find a plane to take me on family business."

"Take that up with Jason. I don't have shit to do with Brewer Air."

"I will. But, for now, I have other, more important—more interesting—things on my plate."

Gannon groans. Again. "Do I even want to know?"

"I'm pretty sure I met my wife today."

Silence.

"Gannon?" I ask, wondering if the call was dropped or if he finally got fed up with me and hung up.

"I'm sorry. Did you say you met your wife?"

"I know it sounds crazy, but crazier things have happened. I mean, it took a matcha latte to bring you and Carys together. But—"

"Tate?"

"Yeah?"

"Get to the point."

I smile as her name coalesces on my tongue. "Her name is Kelly Kapowski."

Gannon's laugh is loud, forcing me to pull the phone from my face.

"What's so funny?" I ask.

*"Her name is Kelly Kapowski?"*

"Yeah ..."

*"Tate."* Gannon does something I've never heard him do. *He cackles.* "Tate, really?"

My brows pull together. "What?"

The humor is still thick in his voice. "Let me get this straight. You met Kelly Kapowski, and now you think you'll marry her? Have you been drinking?"

His amusement is annoying, but I don't dwell on it. As my eldest brother, he's made it his mission in life to either flat-out ignore me or to heckle me in the most frustrating way possible. He's barely more tolerable now that he's married to my best friend.

"No, I haven't been drinking," I say, slipping off my shoes. "We met on the plane and connected. *We had a moment.* I can't explain it."

"I bet you did."

"You know what? I don't like your tone."

He chokes back another laugh.

"Why is this so funny? Renn got accidentally married in Vegas. Jason married his secretary. You married my best friend. And you somehow think that meeting your soulmate on a plane is wild?" I ask. "It sounds like a pretty normal way to meet a woman, if you ask me."

"You know what? Valid point."

"Thank you." I step into the en suite. "Where is Carys? I need her."

"*My wife* is home, and let me reiterate to you for the thousandth time that I don't like you saying you need her."

I ignore him and give the room a quick once-over. After my shower, it's not too messy, but the vanity could use some work. I gather my toiletries and shove them back into my Dopp kit. Then I wipe the counter down with a washcloth. *Much better.* Still, the suite is missing something ...

"Well, *for the thousandth time,* she was my best friend before she was your wife."

"Whatever," he mumbles. "I have a meeting in ten. Give Carys a call. And Tate?"

"Yeah?"

"Ask Kelly if she knows Slater."

"What—"

Gannon's laughter fills the line just before he ends the call.

I roll my eyes as I press Carys's name. As the phone rings, I straighten the pillows on the bed and toss my candy bar wrapper in the bathroom trash. I grab my cologne on the way out and give the pillows a little squirt in case Kelly makes it back to my room tonight. Women usually love a bed that smells like me.

"Hi," Carys says brightly. "Sorry for all the rings. I couldn't find my phone."

*The Situation*

"You, Carys Brewer, have done the impossible," I say, cutting to the chase.

"Oh really? What did I do?"

I open the closet, pull a few things, and lay them on the bed.

"You've started to rub off on your husband," I say, surveying my selections. "The fucker almost has a personality."

"Be nice, Tate."

"I'm always nice. But this isn't about Gannon. I need a favor."

"Sure. What's up?"

"I need your help choosing something to wear tonight."

"At least it's not helping you choose a shirtless picture for Social, I guess."

I roll my eyes. "You are literally the only woman in the world who finds it painful to look at my shirtless pictures."

"Because I know the real you, I've seen a million shirtless photos of your abs, and most importantly, I'm married to your much hotter, much sexier brother."

I make a face as I hit the video call button, and she answers immediately.

"What do I wear tonight?" I ask, flipping the screen so she can see my choices on the bed.

"You called me on the way to the airport."

"So?"

"So how did you get a date in Columbus that fast?"

I swivel the camera, so she sees my face and smile.

"What are you doing?" she deadpans.

"I'm just reminding you who you're talking to."

She glares at me. "Turn the camera around and let me pick your clothes so I can get off here."

"I liked you better before you married Gannon." I turn the camera around again. "I'm meeting a woman at the restaurant downstairs, if that matters."

"Of course, it matters. Where are you staying?"

23

"I'm staying at the Picante hotel. We're having dinner at Ruma downstairs."

"Ooh, I love that hotel. Gannon took me to a Picante in Atlanta a few months ago, and we—"

*Ugh.* "Carys?"

"What?"

"I don't have much time here, so I need this to be about me."

"You are seriously a pain in my ass." She sighs dramatically. "Okay. What kind of vibe are we going for?"

"I want to make her fall in love with me," I say without thinking.

"Well, you aren't going to do that with clothes."

I smirk. "I know. I'll do that after dinner when she rips your carefully chosen outfit off my body."

"Oh my God," she groans.

"But I want to set the stage first. I need to be … irresistible—more than usual." I wince. "Especially because she doesn't know she's meeting me for dinner …"

I cringe at the pregnant pause.

"*Excuse me?*" Carys asks, her voice a couple of decibels higher than usual.

I understand her shock. When I say it aloud like that, it also sounds like a bad plan to me. But that doesn't change how it feels inside me because I'm drawn to her like a moth to a flame. Despite her turning me down … she didn't. Eyes don't lie.

Twisting the camera to face Carys again, I frown. "I asked her out, and she kinda turned me down."

"*What?*" Carys's eyes go wide before she bursts out laughing. "*You got turned down?*"

I glare at her. "It's not funny."

"What happened? How did you manage to get denied? And why are you meeting her if she said no?"

"She said no, but she didn't mean it. If I get there and she did mean it, I'll leave her alone and never talk to her again. But she did let it slip where she would be tonight."

"So you're just going to show up?"

"Yeah. And see what happens."

"What if she shows up with another man?" she asks.

"Great. That'll only help my case."

She pulls her brows together, amused.

"Come on, Carys." I roll my eyes. "Do you really think he'll be better looking than me?"

"I wish I could say no." Her sigh turns into a chuckle. "You better call me afterward. *I'm riveted.*"

"Of course, I will. But it probably won't be until morning because we'll likely spend the night up here." I flip the camera again. "Now, what do I wear? I need to come across … multifaceted. I need to be someone she wants to talk to, but also someone she wants to fuck. I need her to obsess over me like women usually do. Got it?"

She hums as she considers my options. "Okay, no jeans. That's far too casual for the location."

"Agreed."

"Don't do the black pants. That whole ensemble you've put together is a no. I mean, I love it, but it's just not what you want tonight. It screams stuffy businessman and missionary sex."

"We sure as hell don't want that."

"Ooh, I do love you in blue. Get closer to that blazer on top. Is that blue or green? It's hard to tell under the lighting."

I lower the phone. "It's a dark blue."

"Do that. Pair it with the pants lying under it, and … do you have any white T-shirts? The nice ones from Halcyon. Not the ones you work out in."

"Yup." I go to the closet and pull out the shirt in question. "I brought one."

"Yes. Love it. Do that shirt and those pants. Pop a pocket square on the blazer for a little playfulness. I'm assuming you have a belt. And wear your white sneakers, not your dress shoes. That will help it make you look like you tried, but not too much."

"Perfect."

"Great. Do you have anything else I can help you with? Or can I go back to my life over here?"

I return to the main room, pick up the towel from my shower, tidy up the desk, and straighten the chairs by the windows. My computer is on the desk, and I consider putting it away, but ultimately decide to let it stay. It can't hurt for her to see that I'm a professional.

The thought of having Kelly alone in my room makes my skin feel itchy, as if it's too tight for my body. Women don't get under my skin like this. *I'm Tate fucking Brewer.*

Whatever happened today was a bit of a role reversal, but I'm too intrigued by her to care.

"I do have one more thing I need your help with," I say, hanging the towel on a hook in the bathroom. "What flavors do candles come in?"

"What?"

"Don't overthink it. Just give me a few of your favorite candle smells."

She laughs. "My favorite candle *scents*? You're asking me for my favorite candle scents? What's happening right now?"

"I'm trying to arm myself with information."

I sit on the edge of the bed and turn my camera around to look at my best friend. Her brows are pulled together, but she's grinning because she knows me better than anyone. In all the years we've known each other, I've never asked her about candles. I've never given two thoughts about them. The fact that I'm asking—that I want to be able to talk about the things Kelly mentioned she likes—isn't lost on Carys.

Or me. But there's no time to dig too deeply into that.

"What's happening, Tate?" she asks.

"I don't know. I met this woman on the plane."

Carys grins.

"She's the whole package. She's beautiful. Sexy. Funny. She has this ..."

It's more than her sinful body and sweet smile. It's not just her laugh that I can still hear ringing in my ears. I wanted to pull her onto my lap when she touched me.

It's the crazy mix of confidence in her language and vulnerability in her eyes that has me unable to stop thinking about her. And I don't know how to explain that without freaking Carys out. If I said that to her, she'd probably call an ambulance.

"Vanilla is popular," she says softly. "If you want something more manly, you could say you like anything with amber."

"Do I like anything with amber?"

She laughs. "Yes. Your colognes have it."

"Got it. I like amber and vanilla." I stretch my neck back and forth. "I just need some talking points, you know? I want to talk about things she likes, and she mentioned candles. Oh—and romance books. Got any of those for me?"

"Sure do. My current favorite is *Love Hurts* by Mandi Beck. Gannon and I read it to each other some nights."

"*Love Hurts* by Mandi Deck?"

"*Beck*. Mandi Beck."

"*Love Hurts* by Mandi Beck." I close my eyes and repeat it, hoping it sticks in my brain. "Okay, I think that's all I need ... for now, anyway."

Carys smiles. "I can't wait until this date is over so you can call and fill me in. You've piqued my curiosity."

I stand and glance at the time on my phone. "Thanks for your help, but I need to get dressed. Talk to you tomorrow, okay?"

"Okay. Good luck, Tate."

"I don't need luck." I pull the phone away so she sees my abs. "Did you forget who you're talking to again?"

She snorts, shaking her head. "Good night."

"Bye."

I end the call and toss my phone on the bed. My eyes linger on the mattress long after the phone lands.

Excitement stirs in the pit of my stomach. But there's a curious twist in my gut, too. *Because when have I ever been turned down?*

I snatch the phone once again and find Astrid's name at the top.

> Me: Heyyyyyy.

> Astrid: Did the rose arrive?

> Me: Yes, and it's perfect. Thank you.

> Astrid: Great. Now lose my number. 😄

"Rude," I say, tapping out a quick response.

> Me: You don't mean that.

> Astrid: I promise you that I do.

> Me: 😟 I actually need one more thing, and you're the only person who can help me with it because you're brilliant.

> Astrid: Stop trying to charm me, Brewer. I know you. Get to the point.

> Me: I'm going to ignore that.

> Astrid: Whatever works for you. Now, what do you want? I'm organizing a few things for Renn and Blakely's Australian house, and it's a major headache.

"I need to send her something when this is over," I say, then stop and stare at the wall. "Who can I get to send it if she doesn't send it for me? Such a quandary."

I shake my head and refocus.

## The Situation

> Me: Imagine that you came to my hotel room tonight and were impressed. What does that look like?

> Astrid: You would be gone, for starters.

> Me: ASTRID, PLEASE HELP ME. 🙏

> Astrid: Fine. I'm impressed in what capacity? What's the goal here?

I survey the room.

Typically, I don't consider what a room looks like before I bring a woman into it. Because who cares? They're coming for one thing, and that's not to analyze the hotel's housekeeping.

But this time, it matters, and I'm not sure why.

> Me: The goal is to make it feel more comfortable. Make it smell nice.

> Astrid: Tate Brewer, are you trying to be romantic? 😊

> Me: This isn't the kind of woman you take for granted. I gotta up my game. Put in some effort.

> Astrid: You mean *I* need to put in some effort.

> Me: Both of us. We're a team now. 😄

> Astrid: We are definitely not a team. But, because I am impressed at this turn of events, yes, I will help you. How long do I have?

I check my watch.

> Me: Two hours.
>
> Astrid: Damn. I thought Renn's timelines were bad.
>
> Me: I appreciate you.
>
> Astrid: Don't try to suck up now. I've already agreed.
>
> Me: Thank you, Astrid.
>
> Astrid: I gotta go. I have two hours to make magic happen.

I exhale, feeling a little lighter than before. Although she never makes it easy on me, Astrid is brilliant at accomplishing the impossible.

"Now it's my turn to make magic happen," I say, discarding the phone again.

This whole situation has happened so quickly that I haven't had much time to think about the ramifications if she doesn't show up—or, worse, if she shows up at the restaurant with someone else. It wouldn't be surprising if some other man had locked her in for dinner. There's also the tiniest possibility that she's not into me.

I bite back a laugh. *Of course, she's into me.*

Her reasons for turning me down aren't clear, but I suspect I can get to the bottom of it before the night is over.

And, if I'm lucky, I'll get under her before morning, too.

# Chapter Four

## Aurora

I run a towel over my wet hair. My hand trembles, making the process difficult. It's hard to do anything when I'm still buzzed from my interactions with Tate.

*"I really want to see you again, Kelly."*

My knees wobble as I recall Tate's devilish smirk leveled at me.

*How is this happening to me?*

I've floated around my hotel for the last couple of hours, replaying our conversation on the plane and again at baggage claim when we ran into each other.

He offered me a ride to the hotel. I politely declined.

My body still tingles from his hand touching my lower back as he helped me into my ride-share. He wasn't thrilled with my decision to get into the car with the random driver the app sent, and I saw him snap a quick picture of the license plate. I had to finesse my way through the interaction, so he didn't pick up on my real name, and I apologized to Tony, the driver, for Tate's subtle-not-subtle instruction to get me to the hotel quickly, safely, and in one piece.

It was unnecessary. It was also *so* fucking hot.

My phone rings in the bedroom, and I work my fingers through my wet hair as I answer it.

"Hello," I say, putting my intern, Tally, on speakerphone.

"Hi, Aurora. How's Columbus?"

"No complaints so far. What's up?"

"I just wanted to check in and see if you need anything before I leave for the weekend."

"You're sweet, Tally. Thank you for checking on me. I can't think of anything I need, and things here are going great." *My ego is on cloud nine.* "How are things in the office?"

"Good. I finally got the schedule for the stadium gym and forwarded it to you. It's already pretty full through the end of the year, so we might want to reserve slots next week to be sure we have space for tryouts."

I smile. "Smart."

*I'm lucky to be working with her.*

Gaining Tally Thatcher as an intern was an unexpected win. She already had a couple of months' experience working for the team, and we clicked instantly. She's kind and passionate, and her energy makes work fun.

"I also did some digging into community events for the rest of the year and found a few that I think might work great," she says. "Everyone I've talked to has been very receptive to working with us. I'm so excited about how this is coming together."

"That's excellent news. Did you hear back from Charlie about our timeline?"

"Yeah ..." She hesitates, drawing my curiosity. "He came by this morning and asked to meet with us on Tuesday. I got the feeling that something was off."

"Really?" My brows pull together. "Like what?"

"I don't know. He didn't seem upset with us or anything. It was more like his tone hinted something was on his mind that he wanted to say in person. I don't know how to describe it."

I hum, racking my brain for potential issues.

Everything has been going so well. Charlie has shown me nothing but kindness and encouragement, and we've been working seamlessly together. He even said he knew I was perfect for the job as soon as I walked into our interview.

*So what could be the problem now?*

A bubble of anxiety churns in my stomach. I cannot lose this job. Financially speaking, I'd be fine. I can always return to full-time at The Luxe. But money isn't my main objective.

This job fulfills me. It challenges me. *Excites me.*

When one of my clients mentioned that her husband was hiring for a position at his work, and she thought I should apply, I was intrigued. But when I heard what the position was for—that it involved so many things that I loved so much—I was all in. By the time the interview rolled around, I wasn't beyond begging for a chance to prove I was the perfect fit.

Luckily, it didn't come to that.

"I'm sure he just wants a face-to-face update," I say, hoping Tally doesn't worry about this all weekend. "We didn't sit down with him this week. Remember?"

"Yes, I bet you're right." The relief in her tone is evident. "Do you have anything else for me?"

"I don't think so. Go and have a great weekend. Do you have any plans?"

"I'm going home this weekend to train for a pickleball tournament."

"You never fail to surprise me, Tally," I say, laughing.

"Why?" She laughs, too. "You don't see me as a pickleballer?"

"Admittedly, I don't know a lot about pickleball, but I have seen a few videos, and it can get vicious. On the other hand, you are five-foot-nothing and sweet and precious. I can't see you slamming a ball at someone's face."

She giggles. "See? That's my superpower. They see me as this innocent twentysomething and write me off. Then I walk onto the court and rip their hearts from their bodies."

Laughter erupts from me so quickly that I cough.

"That may be a little dramatic," she says. "But you get the point. I'm no pickleball joke. My hometown has a yearly tournament, and I'm the reigning champ for four years straight. I've had different teammates, so clearly, I'm the common denominator."

"Clearly."

"This year's prize is the biggest yet, *and I will win*. But, to do that, I have to teach my boyfriend how to play."

I lean against the counter, amused. "Is he not an athlete?"

"No, he is. He played baseball for the community college. But pickleball is not just about athleticism. You have to have chemistry with your teammate. You have to be able to predict their reactions and trust them to handle their side of the court. A lot goes into it."

"I wish you the best of luck," I say, grinning.

"Thanks, but I don't really need it. I'm a legend."

I can't help it—I laugh again. *This girl is something else.*

"What about you?" she asks. "You have the event tomorrow. What are you doing the rest of the time? Is there a cocktail hour or something?"

*Not exactly, but there could've been cock involved if I would've said yes to Tate,* I think.

I clear my throat and try to decide what to tell her.

Our relationship is 95 percent professional, and I make a concerted effort not to make our conversations too personal. But building camaraderie with your team is essential. She's my right hand and the person I need to vibe with the most. Giving her bits and pieces of me and my life goes a long way.

Besides, I want to tell someone about Tate. I want to share the excitement with another woman that a ridiculously hot guy asked me out, and Jamie didn't answer when I called her earlier. She didn't call me back, either.

*Maddie must have been a handful.*

"Something exciting happened to me today." I shove away from the counter.

"Oh really? Tell me more."

I clear my throat. "I was asked out on a date."

"You what? *Oh my God.* How exciting! Where are you going?"

"Well ... I turned him down."

"*Oh. Why?*"

I wander around the room aimlessly, needing the movement to fight off the excess energy building inside me.

"He was much too young for me," I say. "*Much too hot.* And he had trouble written all over him."

She laughs. "That sounds like a damn good time, Aurora."

*Don't I know it.*

The longer I've been in this hotel room, the more I've started to regret my decision. Sure, I remember why I said no, and I stand by that decision. It was the right call.

But dammit if I keep thinking about what it would be like to see him again—to experience his intense gaze and feel his unmistakable attention and attraction leveled my way. It's been so long since I felt so feminine—desired—and after that small taste, I'd love to experience more.

I *need* more than that, but it would take off the edge. It could be so much fun, too, given the male in mind, and that sounds so appealing. But ...

"So you said no," she says, her voice carrying a tenderness I appreciate. "And now you're kinda wishing you would've said yes. Is that right?"

I blow out a breath. "Yeah. Kind of."

"What was this guy like? Tell me about him."

"He's physical perfection. His personality is a mix of sexy and playful, which makes my brain overheat. He sat by me on the plane, and we had a great conversation. He was just ..." I put a hand to my chest and sigh. "I'm in over my head here, Tally. What am I doing?"

"You are not in over your head." She giggles. "Listen, I know you just got divorced and want to ease your way into dating again, but he doesn't sound like a serial killer or sheep kicker."

"Sheep kicker?" I ask, laughing.

"I didn't get much sleep last night. Work with me."

I laugh again.

"My point is that if you really wanted to see him, what would it hurt? Do you know anything else about him? Is he from Columbus? What does he do for a living? Like, would your paths cross again after this weekend?"

I start pacing again. "I don't think so. He's here for work, but I'm unsure if he's from Nashville or if he was there on a layover."

"Okay, great. Just see this guy while you're there and use it to ease yourself into the game instead of thinking of it *as* the game. Reframe it in your mind. This could be what you were after all along. You just panicked."

I frown. *I didn't panic. I just ...*

*Yeah, I panicked.*

*Oof.*

"Call him," Tally says. "I'm sure he's hoping you will."

"I don't have his phone number. I don't even know his last name." I grimace. "He doesn't even know my real name because I told him mine was Kelly Kapowski."

"Why did you do that?" She laughs. "*Kelly Kapowski?*"

"She was the pretty cheerleader on a show I watched growing up. But that's not the point."

"With all due respect, why are you the way you are?"

I shrug helplessly. "Two divorces will do this to you."

"*Oh my God.*" Tally giggles. "I just searched Kelly Kapowski online. She was a cutie in her little cheerleading outfits while she flirted with Zack—who was hot, by the way. How have I not seen this show before?"

*The Situation*

*Of course, she googled Kelly Kapowski.*

"Speaking of hotties," she says. "You might luck out and see yours before the weekend is over. The world works in mysterious ways, you know."

"Maybe."

"And if you do? Live a little. It's not like he can even look you up if he doesn't know your name. So if he wants to take you to dinner, why not? Why not enjoy the attention and get back into the swing of things? Then you can come home with one adventure under your belt."

*It'd be an adventure, all right.*

"Thanks for the pep talk," I say.

"Anytime."

"Thanks for the call, too. I appreciate you."

"Of course. Good luck this weekend," she says.

"You, too. Good luck with pickleball."

"Not needed! Bye!"

"Goodbye."

I end the call and set my phone on the counter beside my toothbrush.

My reflection shines back at me. Instead of noticing my crow's feet or laugh lines, I see the rosiness of my cheeks. My eyes appear lit from the inside.

*I look happy.*

Since my divorce from Kent, I've done a hundred things to reshape my existence. I've read books, taken yoga classes, and filled my body with healthy vitamins and minerals. There have been girls' nights and wine and paint parties. My wardrobe has been updated with things that make me feel good, and I got a new job that I love.

I've gone through my life with a scalpel, cutting away everything that doesn't fit my new vision for the future. I'm left with a beautiful canvas filled with good things. There's so much room to add to it, too.

*I'm thriving.*

The only glaring hole is my desperate need to be touched.

I reach for a bottle of lotion.

Despite what I was raised to believe, the desire to be touched by another person is a primal human need. I want that connection. I want the passion, the intimacy that I read about in my novels—if even for a night.

*"I really want to see you again, Kelly."*

I set the lotion down as Tally's words come to mind.

*"So if he wants to take you to dinner, why not? Why not enjoy the attention and get back into the swing of things?"*

Blood rushes through my veins as my brain kicks into overdrive, barreling into an area that makes my heart pound faster. I don't know his last name, and he doesn't know mine at all. I did tell him where I was going for dinner tonight, but who knows if he picked up on it?

If he really wants to see me—if the universe thinks we should meet again, he'll be there. *Right?*

I force a swallow, then blow out a long breath, steadying myself.

If he doesn't show up tonight, nothing is hurt. Life goes on. But if he does ...

*"You can come home with one adventure under your belt."*

The idea of seeing Tate again sends a rush of excitement down my spine. I can't remember the last time I felt like this—so ... *alive.*

"Fuck it. What can it hurt?" I snort as I reach for the lotion again. "Famous last words ..."

## Chapter Five

### Aurora

With each step toward Ruma, the restaurant at the end of a long corridor inside Picante, my heels click. Smartly dressed men and women trickle toward me, and I imagine them discussing stock and their summer homes in the South of France—two things I know nothing about. The air of regality and sophistication ruffles my nerves a bit.

*Who are you kidding? Your ruffled nerves have nothing to do with anyone but Tate.*

I take a deep breath and blow it out in an even stream, trying to stop overthinking.

"This is an adventure," I mutter, holding my clutch tightly. "Have fun with it. If he shows up, good. If not, go to the bar and grab a drink. You can pull up a book on your phone if it gets awkward, but it's time to put yourself out there a little bit."

A man with salt-and-pepper hair turns on his heel to watch me walk by him.

I stand a little taller. *Guess this dress was a good choice, after all.*

Two dress options in my suitcase were packed at the last minute, "just in case." I never dreamed I'd pull one out to try to "accidentally" run into a man in the hotel restaurant, or else I might've thought it through a little more. But the one I chose tonight fits me well and checks all the boxes I hope are checked if I happen to see Tate again.

The U-neckline and corseted top of this little black dress makes my boobs look great. The length hits just above the knee, and the slit ending mid-thigh gives it a subtle sexiness that works perfectly. My favorite stilettos and simple gold jewelry make me feel comfortable and pretty.

That's a win.

"He probably won't even show up," I whisper. "Be open to the universe and accept whatever it gives me."

My steps slow as I approach the entrance of Ruma. A small group of stunning college-aged girls stands beside the arched doorway. They huddle together, holding drinks and cell phones, whispering as they not-so-subtly stare ... *at me?*

Before I can turn around, a large palm skims the small of my back, and the contact, combined with Tate's proximity and the warm spiciness of his cologne, lights my body on fire.

My legs wobble as his touch spreads through me like wildfire.

*He's here.*

"Every man out here is staring at you," he says softly behind me, his lips inches from the shell of my ear. "And to think I'm the lucky bastard who gets the privilege of sharing the evening with you."

*Holy shit. Universe, I accept.*

I turn slowly to face him, and his eyes twinkle with mischief.

"Stalking is illegal in Ohio," I say, lifting a brow and trying not to smile.

"It's not stalking if you told me where you're going to be."

"How do you know I'm not here with someone else?"

*The Situation*

He leans down, smirking. "Let's be honest. Even if you were here with someone else, which you aren't, he has a problem on his hands."

"Really? What might that be?"

"Your entire body just reacted when I touched you." He winks, stepping back. "That would be a big problem for him."

I chuckle, my cheeks heating because he's not lying. My body *did* just react to his touch. Goose bumps still ripple across my skin. I don't know what changed between here and the airplane, but the proverbial gloves are off. And all I can think about right now is taking everything else off with them.

"My God, Kelly." He takes another step back, his gaze caressing my body from my face to my stilettos. Every movement feathers the fire burning in my core. "You are an *absolute dream*."

The girls still openly gawking at him might as well be ghosts because I don't think Tate sees them. He's looking at *me*.

All I can do is look at *him*.

Stubble dusts his jawline. A white shirt hugs his body perfectly. Tailored pants highlight his thick, muscled legs, and a deep blue jacket makes his oceanic eyes pop. They're unguarded and undistracted. He's 100 percent present—and downright edible.

"Do you know how beautiful you are?" he asks. "And how *smokin' hot*?"

"Do you realize that there is a pod of girls standing ten feet to your right who are practically drooling over you?"

He lifts a brow. "Really? Then let me wrap my arm around you so you don't slip as we go inside."

I chuckle at his line. *He's good.* But I can't give in this easily.

"Don't you think it's a little presumptuous to assume I'll have dinner with you?" I ask, grinning up at him.

"No."

"And why is that?"

His fingers flex against my hip. "Because I always get what I want."

*God.* "And what is it you want, exactly?"

"You." An easy, cheeky grin kisses his lips as he stares down at me. "This is for you."

A long-stemmed red rose appears out of nowhere.

"You got me a rose?" I ask, surprised and confused. *How did he have time to find a rose?*

"You're adorable."

My brows pull together as he hands me the rose.

"I love that you think I've been able to think about anything other than you." Tate slides his arm around my waist, his fingertips pressing through the fabric of my dress to weigh on my skin. "Let's find our table."

My body tingles at the contact, and I hope he can't feel how my breath stutters. There's no use in pretending I'm not dining with him tonight. We both know it's true.

Tate's fan club's eyes are trained on us as he guides me into the restaurant.

My head spins because, while I hoped I'd run into him, I was not prepared for ... *this*. I hoped I'd run into him, but he's obviously here to try to run into me. To do that, he had to listen to everything I said on the plane and pick up on my dinner plans.

*Is there anything more attractive than a hot man who listens?*

He guides me past a throng of waiting customers and into the restaurant. Heads turn as we pass, all of them admiring Tate—the women longingly and the men admiringly. After a few seconds at the hostess stand, we're ushered deeper inside the establishment. *He made a reservation.*

The vibe is intimate with warm, dim lighting and deep, dark colors. Tall faux plants and strategically placed half walls create private spaces within the building. Candles give off a romantic flair, while gold accents and crystal chandeliers add touches of opulence. The host reaches for a chair, presumably to pull it out for me, but Tate subtly waves him off and does the honors himself. I try not to swoon too hard as I sit, placing my purse and the rose on an empty chair to my right.

A blond man with freckles steps up to our table. "Good evening. My name is Sean, and I'll care for you tonight." He pours two glasses of water. "May I start you off with a drink?"

All eyes are on me.

I'd like a glass of wine, but I'm not confident enough in my wine knowledge to choose something that isn't embarrassing.

"I'll have a vodka soda, please," I say.

"I'll have an old-fashioned," Tate says.

"Could I interest you in an appetizer to start the evening?" Sean asks.

Tate picks up a menu from the table's edge and quickly scans it. "What would you recommend, Sean?"

"Everything is delicious, but my favorite would have to be oysters Rockefeller," Sean says.

"Do you like oysters?" Tate asks me.

I take a menu, too. "I've never had them."

Tate smiles as if this pleases him and turns to Sean. "We'll start with an order of those, beef carpaccio, and your seasonal charcuterie board."

"Fantastic. I'll return shortly," he says before disappearing into the sea of bodies, fake fig trees, and candlelight.

I glance down at the prices and nearly have a heart attack.

"*Tate*," I say, praying he doesn't expect me to pay for half the bill. "*Three* appetizers?"

"I tried to pick three different things since I don't know what you like." His lips twist into a smirk. "But I hope to discover many things you enjoy by the end of the evening."

*Oh God*. I lick my lips and squeeze my thighs together. "I'm not sure that being alone for too long with my stalker is a good idea."

"Don't act like you don't like a little danger."

I laugh. "I don't, actually."

"If you didn't, you wouldn't have casually dropped what restaurant you were dining at this evening."

"That was an accident."

He nods, grinning like he doesn't believe me. "Sure."

"It was," I say earnestly. "I obviously need to be more careful about sharing personal details with strangers."

"Do you want to know what I think, Miss Kapowski?"

"I'd love to know."

His eyes darken as he rests his chin on steepled fingers. "I think—whether you did it intentionally or subconsciously—you told me where you would be, hoping I'd appear tonight. But because you didn't *overtly divulge* this information, you wouldn't feel disappointed if I didn't show up."

*This delicious, insightful bastard. Dammit.*

I hate that he's right, and I hate even more that he knows it. But I'm sure he deals with all sorts of women trying to spend time with him. *Look at him.*

He drags his eyes away from mine and peruses the menu.

"Are you staying in this hotel, too?" I ask, dropping my gaze to the menu, too. Logistics are a much safer topic than my fears.

"My boss knows the man who owns this hotel chain. So we stay in his hotels when we travel, if possible. That's the one thing I will say about my boss. He might be a dick, but he's loyal as hell."

"I doubt I'll be traveling much for my job, but I hope my boss is loyal to nice hotel chains, too."

Tate laughs. "Do you like to travel? Or are you more of a homebody?"

"I've traveled a lot." *Both of my husbands loved to travel, so I pretended to enjoy it, too. Such a waste of time.* "I'm more of a homebody these days."

"Ah, the cozy-girl thing you told me about, right?"

Sean appears again and places our drinks on the table.

"If you aren't ready to order, I can come back," he says kindly.

"Do you have any idea what you'd like, Kelly?" Tate asks.

I bite my lip to keep from reacting to my new faux name. It was a random choice, and I'm confused whenever he says it. I feel the tiniest bit guilty, too. *But what the heck?* It's fun, and tonight is all about that—fun. Admitting that my name is actually Aurora would ruin that.

I scan the offerings and find a chicken dish that only costs an arm, not an arm and a leg.

"The rosemary roasted chicken looks good," I say.

"Excellent choice," Sean says. "It's one of our most popular dishes. I think you'll enjoy it."

"I'll have a filet with peppercorn sauce," Tate says. "Medium rare, please."

"Wonderful. I'll get your order in right away."

We hand our menus over, and Sean marches away.

Tate leans right back into our conversation without missing a beat.

"Tell me more about this cozy-girl thing," he says. "That's what you called it, right?"

"Yeah. I've never had to explain it before." I search for the right words. "It's a vibe, I guess. Instead of living my life in survival mode and just getting through each day, I'm trying to craft a life that feels good. Soft. Feminine. Like my life is wrapped in a fuzzy blanket, if that makes sense."

"You know, I like fuzzy blankets."

I laugh louder than I expect. The statement comes out of nowhere, and something about how he says it is utterly adorable.

"Are you laughing at me?" He chuckles, too. "Men can like fuzzy blankets, you know."

My cheeks ache from smiling. "Men can absolutely like fuzzy blankets."

"And candles," Tate says. "I love candles."

*I bet you do.*

"I really like vanilla and amber," he says. "My colognes usually have those scents."

He grins like the cat that ate the canary.

I'm not sure what he's doing, but it's entertaining, nonetheless.

I sit back and take a deep breath, acknowledging how comfortable I am with him. The openness in Tate's eyes erases some of my nerves, and my shoulders soften as I relax. Like he did on the plane, he whittles down my walls without trying. Although sharing things with him is easy, I need to maintain some boundaries.

"Are you from Nashville?" he asks.

"No."

He waits for me to expound, but I don't.

"What about you?" I ask instead. "Are you from Nashville?"

"Yes. I grew up there. I can't imagine living anywhere else. All my siblings, except my sister, live close to me."

My heart pulls in my chest from the look in his eye. "Family is important to you?"

"Yeah. I mean, it's everything."

He doesn't blink or laugh or crack a smile. Somehow, that might be the sexiest thing about him so far.

"Do you have a lot of siblings?" I ask.

"One sister and four brothers."

"What number are you in the lineup?"

"I'm the baby." He laughs again. "It's all my brothers, then my sister, and then me."

*Oh my God. He's the baby of his family. How old is this guy?*

I take a sip of my drink, hoping the alcohol works quicker than my panic.

Tate leans forward, watching me curiously as I set my glass down.

"Hey, are you okay?" he asks, his voice smooth and calm.

"Of course. Why do you ask?"

"Because you had this flash bolt through your eyes just before you took a drink."

I nibble my bottom lip, and my cheeks burn.

"I'm fine." I smile. "This is just the first meal I've shared with someone in a long time. I just feel a little clumsy."

Tate's eyes are trained on mine. "I assure you, Ms. Kapowski. You are in *very* good hands tonight."

Our gazes lock across the table, and a shiver snakes down my spine. He's a few feet away, too far to touch me. Still, I imagine him between my legs, against my lips, his hands in my hair.

He holds himself with the cool, easy confidence of someone who knows what he has to offer. He speaks with intention. He moves with deliberation. This man understands what he wants and knows how to get it.

*"This could be what you were after all along."*

My breath is shaky as I exhale.

I have a feeling that he's right—I am in good hands tonight. Because if I read the room correctly, I'm what he wants ... and it won't take much to get it.

# Chapter Six

## Aurora

"Enjoy," Sean says before departing from our table.

Our appetizers sit beautifully before us. Each dish is more elegant than the previous one, starting with colorful charcuterie and ending with a spectacular elevated oyster display. It's fancier than anything I've eaten, and my stomach tenses in fear that I won't like it, and it'll go to waste.

"What do you think?" Tate asks, watching me. "Do you think I ordered enough?"

I grin, shaking my head. "I don't know. Maybe you could've ordered two more appetizers, and we could've fed a small country."

He laughs. The sound envelops me with its smooth warmth.

"No, seriously, this is beautiful," I say, surveying the spread again. "But it *is* a lot of food. We could've gotten away with just one of these."

"What kind of date would that have been?"

I fight a grin at his choice of words. "This isn't a date."

"It isn't?" He bites his lip to keep from smiling. "What is it, then?"

"Two random people who met on a plane and happened to run into each other again."

"Is that what you're telling yourself?"

I nod, holding his gaze. "I am."

"We'll see." He pulls his attention to the plates before us. "This does look good."

"I don't even know where to start."

"Always start with oysters." He lifts one from the bed of salt. "You've never had one before?"

"No."

He smiles as if this makes him happy. "Let me introduce you to the world of oysters. You usually eat them with a little lemon or mignonette sauce, but oysters Rockefeller already have a topping on them. You can add a little lemon, but I usually don't."

"What's in the topping?" I ask, peering at the shell in his hand.

"Honestly? I have no fucking idea."

I giggle as he picks up a spoon.

"You can either scoop out the meat and sauce and eat it with a spoon or slip it straight into your mouth." He slides a spoon along the shell. "But either way, you have to loosen the oyster first."

I nod, watching him guide me through the process.

He's deliberate, not rushed or shaky. It's as if he has all the time in the world to sit with me and teach me about shellfish.

His hands are huge compared to the tiny utensil, and his adeptness at handling the oyster makes me wonder what other things he can manipulate as effortlessly. My thoughts instantly switch to his fingers grabbing my thighs and pulling them apart, his face nestled between them, and his tongue licking me instead of his lips.

*Who knew watching this could be foreplay?*

"Now you eat it," he says, holding my gaze.

A quick breath flows between my lips as my heart pounds, and his eyes darken.

He brings the shell to his lips and tips it up, sliding the meat into his mouth. His eyes never leave mine. He chews slowly, watching my reaction, before swallowing.

*Fuck.*

"Want to try one?" he asks, returning the empty shell to the salt bed.

"Absolutely."

He reaches for a new oyster and loosens the insides. "You don't want to swallow right away."

"Says every man I've ever met."

He laughs. "If you chew a few times, it'll help you savor the flavor." He leans toward me, holding the shell across the tabletop. "Come here."

I hitch a breath as chills race across my skin. *He's going to feed me?*

The candlelight casts shadows across Tate's face, making him look even sexier. But now, with his proximity and attention squarely on me, his attractiveness is potent.

There are no distractions and no secondary storylines. His phone is out of sight. He hasn't looked at his watch once. He's here with me in every way, and that's intoxicating.

I part my lips as his eyes blaze. My mouth waters, but it's not for the food.

Tate slides the oyster onto my tongue.

The hit of flavors and textures is powerful and unexpected, as is the warmth of the dish. A rich, creamy sauce mixes with a soft brininess, adding layers of flavor to the buttery topping. But the biggest sensation, the one that steals my breath, comes from Tate's fingers brushing across my bottom lip.

His Adam's apple bobs as he swallows, his eyes glued to my mouth as I chew. Other diners and staff surround us, but they all fade into the background. The moment is wildly intimate. I'm stripped of everything—my clothes, walls, and excuses. And instead of being uncomfortable, self-conscious, or overthinking like usual, I feel powerful.

*Tate is reacting like this to me. Wow.*

"How did it taste?" he asks, a smirk playing against his lips.

"Warmer than I anticipated and not as salty."

He sits back, amused.

I laugh. "It was good. Very interesting flavor, but I like it."

"Did you know that the flavor of oysters is predetermined by where it's harvested?" he asks.

"No. How do you know that?"

"One of my brothers worked in Australia for a while. I visited him, and we learned a lot of things late one night at an oyster bar."

"Did any of those things require an antibiotic?"

He laughs, his eyes twinkling. "Fortunately, no."

"Excellent. So aside from sketchy interactions with shellfish, what else do you do for fun?"

Tate places some carpaccio on his plate. I take a few options from the charcuterie instead.

"What do I do for fun?" he asks, repeating my question. "Honestly, when I'm not working, I like to be home. Most of my friends are married or getting married, so I'm kind of the lone ranger of the group." He takes a bite of his food. "I'm learning to be the fun uncle instead of the fun friend. It's a process."

I spread some honey on a piece of cheese. "I like being at home, too. I love decorating, so I start at one end of my house and work through each room. Once I'm done, I return to the beginning and do it all over again. It can be an expensive hobby."

"I'm terrible at decorating. I just put out a bunch of candles and call it quits."

My eyes narrow suspiciously. There's no way this guy has a closet full of candles, but I'll give him credit for, once again, listening to what I said on the plane and using it to his advantage.

"What about you?" he asks, shifting in his chair. One sleeve pulls back just enough for me to glimpse his thick forearm. "What else do you do for fun?"

*You, preferably.*

"Oh, I don't know," I say, picking up a berry. "I like to cook, I guess. Nothing fancy. I'll see a dish on television, grab the ingredients, and see if I can recreate it—usually with substitutions that ruin it."

He smiles. "My girl Mimi likes to cook."

*Mimi?* I nod as if a streak of jealousy didn't just rip through me.

"Mimi is my brother's wife's grandmother," he says, winking.

I chuckle, knowing damn good and well that he just noticed my reaction. *Again.* I wish that hadn't happened, but it's too late now.

Sean appears again with our entrées. I side-eye the appetizers that we've barely touched.

"You're on it tonight, Sean," Tate says as his steak is placed before him. "This looks great."

"The kitchen is on it tonight," Sean says, setting my chicken before me. "I'm just the deliveryman."

"Well, you're an excellent one," I say. "This looks amazing. Thank you."

"You're very welcome. Can I get you anything else?"

Tate looks at me for approval.

"I'm good," I say. "Tate?"

He smiles and turns to Sean. "Thank you. I think we have everything we need."

"Perfect. I'll swing back by in a few and check in with you. Enjoy."

I sit back and study Tate as he takes a drink. He's such a peculiar man. Attractive, of course, but also equally kind. His manners and genuine respect for Sean, as well as for me, are surprising.

I have so many questions. I can't help but wonder how old he is and what he does for work. He seems to have access to a lot of money and carries himself with a certain confidence that piques my curiosity.

But those questions aren't getting answered, namely because I'm not going to ask. I'm going to keep this light and not dig in too deep. I'm going home tomorrow and leaving him and whatever transpires between us behind.

This is getting me back into the game, not the game itself.

"So this Mimi," I say, slicing into my chicken. "Tell me about her."

"She's the coolest grandma of all time."

"Sounds like you two have a thing."

"Oh, we do." He lifts a piece of steak to his mouth. "And I'm afraid of what that thing would look like if our age gap wasn't a solid fifty years."

I laugh. "Does Mimi have a thing for you?"

"I'll put it to you like this—I see her almost every Wednesday for our date night. That usually consists of dinner that I pick up somewhere and a cookie or cake she makes for me. Then we get into her golf cart, and I drive her, usually shirtless, around the neighborhood so she can make the old man at the end of the street jealous."

My giggles are instantaneous. "You're serious?"

"You've never tasted her lemon meringue pie." He smiles from ear to ear. "She's really ... I wouldn't say sweet because she can be hell on wheels, but we love her. Two of my other brothers and I have adopted her as our pseudo-grandma. She likes me best, of course."

"Naturally."

"I'm going to pretend that I didn't hear the sarcasm in your voice."

"You do that."

We exchange a look that sucks any remaining nervousness out of me.

I can't explain why I feel so at ease with Tate, a man I met only a few hours ago. But I do. He feels oddly safe. He's a breath of fresh, amber-scented air.

The thought makes me chuckle.

We sit quietly and enjoy our meal. We occasionally comment on the taste of our food or the songs playing faintly overhead. Otherwise, we simply share space.

I reach for my drink when a stunning couple stops at our table. The man is older and dazzling with thick, dark hair and intense eyes. The woman on his arm is breathtakingly beautiful in a sleek red dress.

"Fenton," Tate says, standing. "It's good to see you."

Fenton extends a hand toward Tate. "I didn't expect to see you tonight."

The woman looks down at me and smiles warmly. I instantly like her.

"What brings you to Columbus?" Fenton asks.

"I have a conference in the morning. What about you?"

He slides an arm around the woman's waist. "Brynne wanted to see an art exhibit at the museum here this weekend. Tate, have you met my wife?"

Tate looks at her and nods. "I have not. It's a pleasure to meet you, Brynne."

"Likewise," she says.

"Fenton, Brynne, this is my date, Kelly," Tate says. "Kelly, this is Fenton and Brynne Abbott."

My heart leaps at being put on the spot. I have no idea what to do. *Do I stand, too? Shake their hands? Am I supposed to do that double-cheek kiss thing some women do?*

Neither Brynne nor Fenton extends a hand, so I stay seated. Fenton gives me a subtle nod. Brynne, however, turns toward me with a bright smile.

"Are you having a nice time tonight?" Brynne asks as her husband engages Tate in conversation.

"Yes. I've never been here before, and the food is divine. I'm highly impressed."

"Have you chosen dessert yet?" She smirks and glances at Tate. "Aside from the obvious."

I exhale, relieved to be in the presence of a girl's girl. "Not yet."

"Let me suggest the blueberry pie, which, I know, is an odd choice. But Fenton insists that every restaurant he opens in the Ruma chain comes with one dessert unique to that location. The head chef here chose blueberry pie as an ode to the Midwest."

*"My boss knows the man who owns this hotel chain. So we stay in his hotels when we travel, if possible."*

"I just realized that you own the hotel," I say, with a small laugh. "Please pardon what I fear is a look of disbelief on my face."

"How would you possibly know?"

Fenton turns to his wife. "Are you ready, Rudo?"

*Rudo? What does that mean?*

"Yes," she says. "It was nice to meet you, Kelly. Maybe we'll see each other again soon."

"It was nice to meet you, too," I say, withholding my internal commentary that not only will I not see her again, but I won't see Tate, either.

Tate and Fenton exchange goodbyes.

"I'm sorry about that," Tate says, sitting across from me.

"No, it's fine. What an interesting couple ..."

"You have no idea. My brother—I mean, my boss—has been friends with Fenton for a long time. I guess he and his wife have quite the story."

"I got that vibe."

"From meeting them for five minutes?"

I nod.

"How?" he asks.

"You can tell by how they interact with one another. The way they touched so familiarly, and how they spoke so respectfully. There's trust there. Respect." I smile softly. "It was pretty obvious."

I reach for my drink and take a quick sip, my cheeks ablaze.

"Is that the kind of relationship you're after?" Tate asks.

My glass returns to the table as my chest tightens. "Me? No. It probably was at one point."

"Maybe I'm wrong, but being in a respectful, trusting relationship feels aligned with your cozy-girl thing."

I grin at him. "True. But I'm not after a relationship."

"At all?"

"At all." *Not right now, at least.*

He takes his glass and sits back in his chair, sipping his old-fashioned while watching me over the brim. I'm sure he's perplexed by my admission. I'm somewhat surprised by it, too. And the longer we stare at one another, the thicker the tension grows between us.

His question, although unspoken, hangs in the air. My answer, also silent, is on the tip of my tongue. Finally, he leans forward and gives in to his curiosity.

"What are you after then, Miss Kapowski?"

He rests his elbows on the table and peers into my eyes. The playfulness on his lips almost kills me. The intensity of his stare nearly melts me into a puddle on the floor.

My brain comes to a war zone, a clash of what I want and need—two very different things. I need an easy introduction to dating with a sweet and patient guy. But what I want—hell, maybe even what I need at this point—is fucked.

My body temperature rises, a sheen of sweat coats my skin, and a desperate ache grows between my legs. The knot that's been pulling tighter and tighter all afternoon cinches so hard that I nearly grimace. The war zone comes to a screeching halt.

There is a victor.

After all, Tate is the perfect candidate. He's attractive and into me, and I'll never have to see him again. I can be wild and enjoy myself without worrying he'll call me the next day.

*Go for it.*

"I'm looking for one thing," I say, dragging my fingertip around the rim of my glass. "But it would only last one night."

"It's never a one-night stand," he says.

"It would be with me."

"You say that now."

"And I assure you that I'll say that after."

The air grows hotter, tension building rapidly as each second ticks by. He doesn't reply to my statement, and I don't follow up with an explanation. He'll either go into this knowing exactly what my conditions are or return to his room alone.

*Please make the right choice.*

Sean returns, causing me to jump. "Excuse me, please. How are you doing? Can I get you anything else?"

My heart pounds so hard that I can't speak.

Tate drags his eyes away from me as if it pains him. "We're great."

"Mr. Abbott has paid your bill this evening, and I have been asked to serve you our famous blueberry pie for dessert. Would you like that now?"

Tate looks at me again with a fire so hot in his eyes that I nearly whimper.

*What can this hurt? It's just one night because he doesn't even know my name.* I lick my lips. *It'll be one hell of an adventure.*

I hold Tate's gaze. "Sean, can we get that pie to go?"

Tate's eyes darken, and he stills.

"Absolutely," Sean says. "Let me grab that, and I'll be right back."

"Thank you," I say sweetly.

Tate removes his wallet and pulls out a few hundred-dollar bills. He tosses them unceremoniously onto the table.

"So you're just looking for tonight, huh?" he asks.

"That's it."

"What should I do when you call me in the morning?"

I grin. "I don't have your number and won't ask for it. So that won't be a problem." I study him closely, and he almost looks … disappointed. *Surely, he's used to this type of arrangement.* I don't want to ask the question rolling around my head, but the words slip past my lips before I can stop them. "What are you after, Tate?"

He holds my gaze unabashedly.

"The mother of my children," he says without apology.

The words, *the idea*, burst through my veins and pool in my core.

I'm not one to be turned on by the thought of having a child, but it's insanely hot coming from him. Instead of looking for the next warm body or a good time, he's looking for a family.

*He's too good to be true.*

"I'm not her," I say. "But I can provide you with a distraction."

He licks his lips. Before he can reply, Sean is back like a bad habit.

"The note said to bring you an entire pie," he says. "I put it in a box for you."

Tate hands Sean the cash he had tossed on the table. "Thank you for your service this evening. You were great."

"Yes, thank you," I say.

"I appreciate that." He dips his chin. "Can I get you anything else?"

Tate shakes his head. "I think we're calling it a night. Thanks again."

"Have an enjoyable rest of your night," Sean says.

Tate stands, stalking around the corner of the table like a predator on the loose.

I hitch a breath, holding it as his fingertips slide across the top of my exposed back. A chill races down my spine at the contact, and I struggle not to moan. He pulls out my chair, and I get to my feet, bringing my rose and purse with me as I rise.

He's a wall of muscle behind me as his lips lower to my ear.

"Are you ready to get fucked, Miss Kapowski?" he whispers just loud enough for me to hear.

"My room is across the hotel."

"Mine is directly above us."

"Yours, it is."

His laugh is low as he takes my hand, laces our fingers together—grabs the pie—and guides me out of the restaurant.

# Chapter Seven

## Tate

"Oh, wow," Kelly says as she enters my hotel suite.

I let the door close softly behind me, then scan the room myself. *Wow, indeed.*

Astrid outdid herself.

A massive bouquet of deep red roses, matching the one I gave Kelly, has been placed on the center of the coffee table. The lights have been slightly dimmed, creating a moodier backdrop for the flickering candles scattered on various furniture pieces. Faint music—light but sexy—sets the perfect atmosphere.

Kelly moves gracefully across the room, and naturally, my eyes are glued to the curve of her hips beneath the soft black fabric of her dress. *Fuck, she's gorgeous.* My fingers have itched to dip beneath the hem—to feel her smooth skin against my palms—since I spotted her in front of Ruma. There's so much to explore with her, on her, and inside her, and I want to experience it all so badly I can taste it.

"Remember when we were on the plane and you asked me whose side I was on?" Kelly glances at me over her shoulder. "You or your boss's?"

"Yeah."

"I told you then I was neutral." She winks. "But I've changed my mind. I'm on your boss's side now."

"Excuse me?" I chuckle, tossing the blueberry pie on the sofa. It hits the cushion with a thud. "That sounds like a challenge."

She shrugs, peering across the darkened city. "This view is amazing—much better than my little window looking out on the rooftop of the building below." She laughs softly. "If your company is ever hiring, remember me."

I fight a smile. "I do have quite a bit of pull." I step behind her, lowering my mouth to her ear again. "And I can be *very* persuasive."

Goose bumps spread across her skin like wildfire. She hitches a breath, her body leaning against mine as if on instinct. I press my erection into her so she can feel how hard I am already.

"I have a feeling that you don't have to work too hard to get what you want from people," she says, moving her ass slowly against me.

I suck in a breath through my teeth.

Her perfume scents the air, taunting me with its warmth and sweetness. It triggers a need to touch, to connect. Every cell in my body is drawn to her, and I fear I'll be unable to satisfy this craving.

But I don't want to give in ... yet.

Delayed gratification makes things so much better.

"Would you like a drink?" I ask, turning toward the small kitchenette near the door—needing to put some distance between us. *My cock hates me right now.* I remove two champagne flutes from a small tray that Astrid arranged. "I have champagne, and it looks like a bottle of red wine."

An amused grin slips across her lips. "Do you always have a convenient bottle of champagne in your work suites? And a bouquet of roses?" She glances at the buds exploding from the vase in front of her. "And candles?"

"I do when I ask for them."

She nods slowly, and I can see the wheels turning in her head.

I'm sure she's wondering how the pieces of this puzzle fit together because I'm supposed to be a regular, but extremely handsome, guy. But regular guys wouldn't have the means to pull all this off. I can do it because of my bank account and Astrid. But I can't tell Kelly that. I *can't* answer the questions rolling around her brain because she'd learn my last name. She'd know I'm a Brewer. While I'm not embarrassed by that, many people associate it with our dad now—and we're guilty by association. That's one battle I don't want to fight tonight.

"Let me get this straight," she says, resting her hip against a chair. "You get to the hotel this afternoon, and find God knows how many roses. Then you order champagne before waiting outside of Ruma?"

"No." I fill two flutes with champagne and then cross the room to her. "I also made reservations at Ruma, got in a quick workout, and worked a little."

She takes a drink from me. "That's a lot of work."

"It's already paid off."

She lifts a brow, taking a sip.

"My objective was to see you again, Miss Kapowski. Anything beyond that is icing on the cake."

"I'm not sure whether to be flattered or concerned."

My lips twitch. "Be both. It's healthy to keep a small amount of skepticism about things."

"Oh, I wouldn't call my level of skepticism small."

"About me?"

She shrugs. "About you, yes. About men in general. Life. Everything, I suppose."

"Want to tell me what that's about?"

She pushes off the chair so she's facing me squarely. "I came here for one reason, and that isn't to discuss philosophical views on life."

I set my drink on the end table.

Kelly looks up at me through her thick, dark lashes, peering into the depths of my soul. I study her just as deeply. I wish I knew her better—what she likes, what makes her tick. *What are her points of vulnerability? What does she need from me?* I've never really asked myself these questions about a woman, and certainly not one I've known for less than twelve hours.

But that's a thought for a different day.

"Can I ask you one question?" she breathes.

"Absolutely."

"How did you know when to make the reservations at Ruma?"

"Simple. I reserved a table for the whole evening."

"They let you do that?" Her eyes nearly fall out of her head. "I've worked in the restaurant business. That's not a thing at a high-end establishment on a busy evening."

*It is when you're me.* "It was a thing tonight."

She tears her gaze from mine, hiding a smirk as she moves to the wall of windows once again.

"How were you there the moment I arrived?" she asks, facing the glass.

"The lobby has a clear view of the corridor leading to Ruma."

"So you just sat there and waited on me?"

"I mean, I stood some of the time."

She looks over her shoulder, and the look she gives me could start a forest fire. The gentle curve of her lip hints at mischief. There's a knowing glint in her eyes. Her head slightly tilts to the side in a playful invitation.

I remove my jacket and toss it onto a nearby chair.

"You stood some of the time?" She laughs softly. "Who sits in a lobby with an open reservation just hoping someone walks by?"

I hold her gaze. "Someone who knows what they want."

"And you want me?"

"You have no fucking idea how much I want you."

My voice is rough and gravelly, and her lips part as the sound

*The Situation*

reaches her. My body tenses with anticipation. I can feel my heart pounding in my chest.

Kelly turns to face me. Candlelight dances in the reflection behind her, enveloping her in a warm glow. The amusement from moments ago is gone, and in its place is *lust*.

"I've had a very shitty two years," she says, her gaze boring into mine. "I want you to make me forget about it. Think you can do that?"

*Motherfucker.*

"Yes, ma'am," I say, smirking. Then I nod to the drink in her hand. "Finish it or get rid of it."

She grins devilishly before downing the rest of the champagne.

I take the empty glass from her and place it next to mine.

"Now come here," I say.

I take her hand in mine and pull her roughly to me. Her eyes go wide as she lands against my chest. Rapid breaths press her tits against me—round and perfectly sized for my mouth. Her dark eyes catch mine, wild and unmasked, like she's struggling to anticipate my next move.

My body's reaction to her is swift and violent—every inch buzzes with the need to take her. It requires every bit of restraint I can muster not to throw her over the back of the couch and fuck the hell out of her.

But that would be too fast. Too selfish. Too hedonistic.

I must stay in control.

I'll take my pleasure tonight in pleasing her.

"I'd love to have you on your knees with my cock in your mouth," I say, pressing the pad of my thumb across her lips.

She nips her teeth against my skin, and the nip pulses through every cell inside me.

*Dammit.*

"Turn around for me." I grip her hips unabashedly, spinning her slowly until she's facing the other way. "This is like unwrapping a present."

I drag her zipper down her back in one slow and steady tug. It stops at the top of her ass.

My mouth waters as I lazily appraise the curve of her hip and flawless skin.

No panties.

*Fuck.*

My cock throbs so hard that I wince.

"Every time you touch me, I think I'm going to fall apart," she says, her voice breathless.

"That's exactly why you aren't touching me. I'd explode."

She shivers as the top of her dress falls forward. I grip her waist again, my heart thrashing at the contact. I press myself against her back and my cock strains to touch her, bulging against my pants.

Her head falls onto my shoulder, and she brings her arms above her head and drapes them over my shoulders to the back of my head. My hands slide to her front—across the dip of her hip, rounded stomach, and up to her full tits.

"Fuck," I groan, the lace of her bra rough against my palms. "Has anyone told you how fucking sexy you are?"

"Not in a long time."

"I don't believe that."

"Then don't." She plays with the hair at the nape of my neck. "I want to come so bad."

I glide my hands to her back. It takes some work, but I unclasp her bra without looking.

"You will," I say as the lace falls to the floor. "Patience is a virtue."

"The fact that I haven't shoved you to the couch and climbed you like a tree demonstrates my patience," she says, her eyes fluttering closed. "But I'll warn you, it's running low."

I cup her tits in my hands, and the weight of them sends a shock of electricity to my dick.

"What's your favorite way to come?" I ask, pressing a kiss to the crook of her neck.

## The Situation

She tilts her head, offering me full access. "I forget."

"What do you mean?" *How does a beautiful woman like this "forget" how she likes to come?*

"It's been a while." She arches her back as soft moans escape past her lips. "I've been getting myself off for eighteen months. Before that, I was finishing the job myself most of the time, too."

"Are you serious?"

She nods, grinding her ass against my cock.

I pick my jaw up and formulate a plan. While I don't know her backstory, it's obvious someone has screwed her over. That was why she hesitated to meet me tonight and didn't answer any of my personal questions.

That's also why she only wants to fuck.

I grin.

*You've come to the right place, Kelly Kapowski.*

I am going to rock her world so fucking hard that she'll want even more than my number.

She'll want me.

# Chapter Eight

## Aurora

Tate's hands slide over my hips and shove my dress down my legs. His palms rub against my skin—fingers splayed, tips dragging behind so deeply it almost hurts.

I'm lightheaded despite being anchored in the moment, and every sense is overstimulated.

The air is thick and musky, making it hard to breathe, and Tate's breath on my neck feels like flames licking my core. My thighs are sticky.

It's too much. It's also not nearly enough.

"Breathe," Tate whispers into my ear. "You have to breathe, gorgeous."

I exhale, releasing the breath I've been holding.

*How am I even here?*

I never expected to find such a ... stimulating experience again, and especially not with a man so much younger than I am. With so much more experience, too, it seems. A man who doesn't even know my real name.

I'm about to fuck a man I'll never see again after tonight.

*Who am I?*

"Step out of your dress," he says, brushing my hair across my shoulder. "Heels stay on."

I step one foot and then the other, holding his hand for balance.

"Now turn around and face me."

Tate boldly rakes his eyes over the length of my body as I face him. His gaze is slow and seductive, and I can almost feel it slide over my curves. It's as if he's mentally photographing every dip and freckle, cataloging them like precious goods.

"Fuck, Kel. You're even sexier than I imagined."

I'm intoxicated, high on hits of dopamine.

I somehow forgot that I could elicit this type of reaction from a man. I'd gotten comfortable with the idea of being forty, and that no man would find me young and beautiful. It never crossed my mind that someone would ever still see me like the twentysomething I feel I am on the inside.

Until now.

"My God," he says, licking his bottom lip. His eyes finally lift to mine, and they're hooded. The corner of his lips curls into a devious grin as he takes a few steps back. "We're going to have so much fun tonight."

I swallow through the constriction in my throat and take one step toward him. Then another, bolstered by his reaction. Each movement is deliberate—the click of my heel, shift of my weight, jiggle of my breasts. He watches me with rapt attention, his eyes never leaving my body.

My hands skim beneath his shirt and discover a wall of muscle. They roam up to his chest and over his shoulders, appreciating every ridge and valley of his chiseled physique. He flexes against my touch, sending a shiver down my spine.

Tugging the shirt over his head, I expose his body inch by delicious inch, causing me to squeeze my thighs together as I witness, for the first time, the epitome of male perfection. *Damn.*

"I've only seen bodies like this online, and I swore it was all photoshopped," I say, openly gawking.

"And you haven't even gotten to the best part," Tate says, winking.

I grab his waistband and yank him to me.

"Getting aggressive, Miss Kapowski?" he asks, watching me undo his belt.

The name makes my stomach knot, and I wish I could correct him. I'd love nothing more than to hear him call me Aurora. It would make this that much hotter, and I'd feel far less guilty. *I'm giving him my body, but I can't give him my real name?*

I can't fix this now. There's no way. Besides, by this time tomorrow, he'll only be a memory. *What does it really matter?*

"Does my aggressiveness intimidate you?" I tease.

"Oh, no. Please don't hurt me. That would be *awful*," he deadpans.

"Don't be a smart-ass."

His chuckle cuts through me like a hot knife. "I think you misunderstand this situation."

"What makes you say that?" I slide his belt out of his pants and toss it to the side. Then I palm his cock through his pants and look up at him. "This is kind of hard to misunderstand, isn't it?"

His hand covers mine, his fingers pressing mine harder against him.

"The part you don't seem to comprehend is that I'm here to please you," he says. His eyes, aroused, are more green than blue. "Whatever gets you off is what I'm into." He leans forward until his lips hover above mine. "Don't be confused about that, either. Because, by morning, you will know every way you can come."

*Good God.*

I suck in a breath as he pulls away from my face.

*The Situation*

His words stoke the inferno sizzling inside me, a fire that's hotter and brighter than I've ever felt before. Life is breathed into me again. Each touch, word, and look brings me closer to a version of myself I thought was long gone, having faded away with my failed relationships.

My hands tremble as I unfasten his pants. The hiss of his zipper kisses the air as I lower it one tooth at a time. It's a moment pregnant with anticipation and thick with tension, and I focus on the proximity of my hand to his cock.

Tate's fingers brush across my cheek before he turns, removing his socks and shoes, and then his pants and briefs. His back ripples with each movement, each muscle flexing and pulling in a spectacular show just for me. Finally, he turns to me with his cock in his hand, and my eyes instinctively follow the movement.

*Holy. Fucking. Hell.*

He strokes himself from root to tip. A bead of pre-cum has already gathered on the head. His shaft is thick and nearly as long as his hand—*and I want it inside me.*

"I think you're the one misreading this situation," I say.

"Really?"

"You don't seem to comprehend that I want you to bury yourself inside me." I lift a brow. "*Now.*"

His eyes widen, and a slow smile splits his lips. "Get over here."

He cups my face with both hands a split second before his mouth covers mine. It happens so fast that I'm unprepared. I gasp a breath before slinging my arms over his shoulders and running my fingers through his hair, *melting into him.*

His lips are soft and full, and each kiss is demanding and intentional. They press and glide against mine—guiding them in a dance that feels like we've practiced many times before. His tongue slips into my mouth, parting my lips as if he owns them.

I whimper and sag against him.

A dizzying current rushes through my veins and coalesces in the apex of my thighs.

"Tate," I moan as he presses kisses along my jaw.

He picks me up and I wrap my legs around his waist. My heels drop to the floor, and his cock slides against my pussy, taunting it. *Taunting me.* My head falls back as I thrust my hips against him, begging for friction. Contact. *Relief.*

"You promised me orgasms," I say, moaning every time the head of his dick touches my clit.

"Do you want to come on my face or cock first?" He carries me into the bedroom, nipping my bottom lip between kisses. "Tell me."

I shake with anticipation and from the forwardness of his question. I've never been asked this before. Sex has never been about me, and I've certainly not been given options.

"Face," I say, as mine turns red.

"Excellent choice."

He kisses me long and hard before tossing me on the bed. I squeal, the sound turning into laughter that's silenced by Tate crawling across the mattress like a predator on the prowl.

My belly tightens as he comes to a stop in front of me.

"You have the best tits I've ever seen," he says, holding them in his palms. "Perfect shape. Perfect weight." He flicks one nipple with his tongue, and it beads for him immediately. "So responsive."

I hold the back of his head as he sucks the bud through his lips. The warmth and wetness of his mouth against my breast, and his fingers lightly pinching the other, disarms me. I slip a hand between my legs and gasp at how wet and hot I really am.

"*Stop.*" He pulls back, gripping my wrist and withdrawing it from my groin. His eyes blaze. "Don't."

"I'm desperate," I say, shivering.

"All of your orgasms are mine tonight." He lies down, his head flat on the bed. His cocks stands at full attention. "Get over here and ride my face until you come."

His words alone nearly make me come undone.

"Are you sure you won't smother to death from this?" I ask.

"Can't think of a better way to go out."

I roll my eyes as I reach him.

"Straddle me and grab the headboard," he says.

My brain screams, and I can hear the echo, but even that doesn't stop me from putting one knee on either side of Tate's head.

"If I die," he says, grinning, "just know I went out at the peak of my existence."

"Shut up," I say, laughing.

"You can shut me up by sitting down and grinding your pussy on me."

*Ho-ly fuck. I'm really doing this.*

I look down to see his eyes are nearly feral.

*You only live once ...*

I grip the headboard with both hands and hover over Tate. His tongue parts me, licking a long, lazy stroke through my pussy.

"*Oh God.*" I shudder.

It's been too long. There's too much pent-up sexual frustration to make this last. I'm on the verge of spiraling over the edge, and we've only just begun. I'm too close to breaking into a million pieces to worry about what I'll look or sound like when I lose control.

"Take your time." Tate's fingers bite into my thighs. "We're in no hurry." He drags his tongue through me again. "I'm happy to lie here and eat you all night. This is all about *you.*"

"*This is all about you.*"

God.

I close my eyes and begin to move my hips, rocking back and forth in the most delicious, leisurely motion. Tate matches my rhythm with his tongue, stroking against my swollen flesh.

"*This is so good,*" I say, the pleasure so intense it's nearly pain.

His palms move to my ass, massaging my cheeks and pulling me tighter to his face. I lower myself just a touch, enough to increase the friction by a hairsbreadth. It's perfection—just the right amount of pressure to make me delirious and hold me back from descending into orgasmic bliss.

The thought of Tate's mouth on my pussy—the sounds of him

kissing and stroking my slit like it's a fucking dessert—makes my head spin.

"Just like that." I rock harder against him, my head falling back. "Fuck me just like that."

He clamps down on my ass, holding me in place, and sucks my clit. It's intense and electrifying, and I yell out as explosions rocket through my body.

"Tate!" I virtually scream, squeezing my eyes shut as bursts of colors nearly blind me. "Oh my God! *I'm coming so fucking hard.*"

I tremble, literally shaking against his face as he continues the decadent onslaught. My thighs are soaked. My breath is stuck in my chest. A full-body shudder slams through me as the sound of Tate sucking and licking fills the air.

I try to lift, but he pulls me down, holding me tight against his face. I sag against the headboard, moaning but unable to stop moving.

*It feels too good.*

Finally, his movements slow, and I'm able to lift off him. Tate assists my dismount and lays me next to him, his breathing as ragged as mine. He rolls onto his side and grins, licking the evidence of my orgasm off his lips.

"I'm going to go out on a limb and say you enjoy coming that way," he says, his eyes twinkling.

I sink into the mattress, giggling. "What was your first clue?"

"You drenched me." He chuckles, wiping his face with the sheet. "That was seriously the hottest thing I've ever done. *Ever.*"

My cheeks flush. *Right.* I don't care that he's probably said that to a thousand girls. He can say whatever he wants as long as he keeps delivering orgasms like that.

"Well, I can say with absolute certainty that nothing I've ever done has come close to that," I say. "Face riding is officially my favorite way to come."

"Don't make that call this early in the night."

*This early in the night?*

My limbs are exhausted, and my needs are more than met. They're exceeded. But Tate, in all his youth, is still raring to go.

"Look, I don't know—and don't want to know—what kind of sex life you have," I say. "But my stamina is apparently depleted because I'm dead."

He sighs, shaking his head. "Sorry."

"Sorry?"

He breaks out into a smile and hops off the bed. "You have about ... eh, I'll say three minutes to figure out how to reenergize yourself."

"What are you talking about?"

He slides his hand down his shaft and grins. "I'm going to go wipe your pussy juices from my face and grab a condom. Then we'll see how doggy style ranks." His grin bleeds into a smirk. "Told you I could make juices sexy."

I grab a pillow and halfheartedly throw it at him.

He laughs all the way to the en suite, leaving me to die alone.

*But, oh, what a way to go.*

I'm just getting my blood pressure back to normal when he waltzes into the room with the energy of a twenty-something-year-old man. *Fitting.*

"Over here," he says. "Ass up. Let's go. Move it."

The fire in my core begins to reheat. "I just learned something new."

"What's that?"

"I can't reenergize myself," I say, rising slowly and moving to him. "But you can reenergize me pretty damn easily."

"Good to know."

He takes my face in his hands and kisses me like he means it. His skin is damp from the washcloth, and his mouth is hot. I can taste myself on his tongue. Even that turns me on.

*Wow.*

Suddenly, I'm horny all over again.

He flips me onto my stomach, then reaches under me and lifts. I'm on all fours, looking at him over my shoulder, as he takes his cock and lines it up with my opening. I hold my breath, not sure if he's going to go slow or give me a moment to acclimate to him.

"I—*oh fuck!*" I say as he slides all the way inside me.

I sink back, squeezing my eyes shut as my body accepts his girth.

"You're so damn tight." His words are strangled. "I'm going to give it to you hard." He pulls out and slides in again, slower this time. "Are you ready?"

*That's a complicated question, sir.*

I ball the sheets up in my fists and brace myself. "Fuck me hard, Tate."

"*Damn you.*"

He grips my hips, his fingers digging so deep he finds my bones. He draws his cock out in a single, lazy pull. I start to relax and take a breath when he buries every inch of himself deep inside my pussy.

"Ah!" I yell, blinded once again by the intensity of Tate's movements.

He slams into me repeatedly in long, delicious strokes. I meet him thrust for thrust, greedy for the pops of bliss each time the head of his cock hits the back of me.

"I love this," I say, my voice broken by each wave of pleasure. "This is so, so good." I arch my back. "*Oh yes.* Right there. Harder."

"Your pussy is gripping my cock so fucking tight."

My core tightens again as another climax gathers. "I'm going to come again."

"Do it. Come on my cock, Kelly. Bust all over me, gorgeous."

I hiss as the buildup hits a boiling point, and I teeter on the edge. My arms tremble, giving out until I'm held up on my elbows. I arch my back, lifting my hips and inviting him to fuck me even harder.

"There!" I shout, meeting him thrust for thrust. "*There, Tate!* Right ... fucking ... there."

My face plants into the comforter as wave after wave crashes over me. Tate holds me up by my hips, refusing to let me deny myself any part of my orgasm. Being held and forced to absorb every drop of my

*The Situation*

climax is an act all of its own. I will think about this, reliving it over and over, for the rest of my life.

Tate slowly eases his tempo until he's no longer moving at all. He stills, his cock buried inside me, then massages my ass cheeks.

"This ass is perfection," he says, smacking me lightly. The sound cracks through the room, which, in turn, reignites the fire smoldering in my core. "I'd like to fuck this."

"My ass?" I yelp.

He laughs. "I'll take that as a no."

"Hard no." *Well, maybe. At this point, I'd probably love it, too.*

He pulls out and guides me gently to the mattress. I flop onto it in a very unsexy way. But I can't help it. Every limb is jelly.

"I think you liked that one, too." He chuckles.

I try to answer him, but the words are a muffled mess.

"I'm two for two," he says. "Now come on. Let's see if we can go three for three."

He can't be serious. I know I talked a good game and I've dreamed of a man who can't get enough of me, but this is definitely biting off more than I can chew. I'm so, so wonderfully spent.

I don't know who I am or how I got here, exactly, because nothing in my life would lead me to believe that I'd find myself in a stranger's bed in postcoital bliss—especially an impossibly sexy stranger like Tate. But this is what I needed, and it's better than anything I could've imagined. I'm protected by my anonymity. I'm free to indulge, enjoy, and explore.

To have an adventure ...

"Roll over," he says, helping me flip onto my back.

He's peering down at me with a sweet smile when I open my eyes, which does things to my heart that I choose to ignore.

"Are you tired?" he teases. His features are so bright, so clear. It's impossible not to smile at him.

"What does it look like to you?"

"What does it look like to me?" He tilts his head to the side. "It looks like you're far less stressed than you were this afternoon." He runs a hand up the inside of my thigh, setting off a firework display inside my belly. "And you look even more beautiful lying naked on my bed, spread out just for me."

I glance down to see his cock still rigid. Still needing a release. Still ready for *me*.

"How did you not come from that?" I ask. "I've gotten off twice, and you ... haven't?"

He scoots me up to the middle of the bed.

"I didn't come because I wanted to ensure you were satisfied," he says. "And when I get off, I want to be looking at your pretty face. Not that your ass isn't amazing."

I laugh, blushing.

"But I want to see you." He winks at me as he spreads my legs and places himself between them. "Is this okay?"

*What kind of question is that?*

"This is perfect," I say, spreading wider for him. "I want to watch you fall apart, too."

And I do.

Even though I've often loathed it when a man hovers over me when he gets off, mostly because I've not gotten close to a release, I *need* to see this man fall apart.

Tate puts a hand next to my head before positioning himself once again at my opening. He enters me slowly this time, sinking into me inch by precious inch.

I moan softly as he hovers over me, moving in and out in a lazily perfect rhythm.

His mouth lowers, his eyes searching mine. My heart swells in my chest as I lift my head, meeting him suspended in the middle. He takes a quick breath before capturing my lips with his.

This round is different from the others. It's not less or more, just not the same. It's without the fire and passion of the first two. Instead, it's sweeter with more connection.

Although I have absolutely no business leaning into this version of sex with him, I can't help myself.

I wrap my arms around his middle, feeling the sheen of sweat coating his skin and his muscles flexing.

Just as my core tightens and that now familiar fire begins to catch, Tate's body begins to tremble.

"Come," I whisper, tilting my hips to get the best angle possible. "I'm ready to come again, too."

"Fuck."

He groans, the sound starting deep in his throat and shaking as it passes his lips. I fight to keep my eyes open as my third orgasm of the night sweeps through me.

Tate's Adam's apple bobs as the vein in his temple pulses like I saw on the plane.

He pounds into me harder and as deep as he'll fit, as sweat drips from his forehead onto my chest. He groans again, his face turning red as the climax reaches him.

"Dammit," he says through gritted teeth.

He sinks into me all the way, holding himself there as he fills the condom with his seed. My body heats as I hold my chest in both hands and moan his name. Back arched. Eyes closed. Pussy firing on all cylinders.

"Does that feel good?" I whisper, squeezing my muscles around him. "It feels so good to me, Tate."

Finally, he blows out a breath as the last bit of my orgasm fades away. I open my eyes to find his waiting for me.

"Wow," I say.

He grins in return as he pulls out of me. "I was going to ask you if that was as good for you as it was for me, but there's no way."

"Oh, there's a way." I giggle. "You're three for three."

He laughs. "So you were reminded that you enjoy oral, doggy style, and missionary?"

"No."

His brows pinch together.

"I discovered *I love* all three of those things when delivered like you just did," I say as he lies beside me. "I've never experienced anything like that before."

He presses his lips together and withholds whatever's going through his mind. It doesn't matter. I know he's pleased with himself—as he should be.

"You said you wanted a bath with candles after dinner," he says, lightly drawing a line down the center of my chest. "I have a bathtub *and* candles."

"So prepared."

"I do aim to please."

*You do a damn good job of it.*

He hops off the bed and removes the condom.

His body flexes—taut, tanned, and strong. He's a total work of art.

*When will I ever get to do this again? When will I ever find myself in bed with a man nearly half my age who is not only willing but also eager to do things to me that no man has ever done before?*

I take a deep breath, fighting the uptick in my heartbeat.

"I'll get a bath running for us," he says, stretching his arms overhead. The candlelight casts a sexy shadow over him. "But don't come into the en suite until I tell you, okay?"

"Hey, Tate?"

"What, gorgeous?"

*Fuck it.* "How about we forget the bath and see if you can go four for four?"

His smirk is sinful.

A delicious shudder heats my body, and my heart flutters wildly. *Madly.* This is the romance-novel passion I've dreamed of experiencing. It's intense and passionate—potentially destructive, but that's a dark moment I'm willing to push off until later.

The climax is *so* worth it.

"Do you have anything in mind?" he asks as his cock hardens before my eyes.

*The Situation*

I gulp, my face flushing. "I've always wanted to try reverse cowgirl."

He chuckles as if he can't believe my request.

"Are you laughing at me?" I lift a brow.

"I'm wondering how I got so fucking lucky."

"Well, it's probably—*ah!*"

I burst into a fit of giggles as he leaps on the bed and covers my body with his. His lips find mine, and he swallows the laughter, leaving me breathless.

Again.

It turns out I do, in fact, like anything this man does to me.

# Chapter Nine

## Aurora

*Ouch!*

I straighten my legs beneath the sheets and wince again.

*Why am I so sore?*

I crack my eyes open to the bright morning sunlight streaming in from a small opening in the windows. *Hotel windows.*

*Oh, right. I'm in Columbus for the conference.*

*The conference!*

*Shit!*

My eyes fly open. They only grow wider as the events of last night come barreling back to me. Slowly, I turn my head to the right.

*Oh my God.*

*I'm in his bed.* I peek under the sheets. *Still naked.*

*At least he's naked, too. And half hard. Is Tate ever not ready to go?*

## The Situation

My core constricts, craving another round with the man who wore me the hell out last night.

But there's no time for that.

I glance at the clock on Tate's side of the bed and breathe a tiny sigh of relief. I have two hours to get ready for work—the actual reason I'm here.

*This was a one-night stand, Aurora. Don't lose the plot.*

Guilt swamps me as I lie in a stranger's room, blissed out from a night of sex instead of being focused and prepared for today's events. Now I have to do a walk of shame to my room and hope I don't see anyone I'll meet later today, because it'll be obvious what happened. No one is wearing the dress and heels I'll be wearing this early in the day.

Or looking so thoroughly fucked.

I rub my forehead, trying to slow my thoughts down.

*I have to get out of here.*

After a glance at Tate's chiseled abs and sexy shoulders, I climb out of bed as quietly as I can.

I tiptoe into the living area, closing the bedroom door softly behind me, and gather my discarded heels as I go. My dress is where I stepped out of it last night. I do a brief search for my bra to no avail.

"Forget it," I whisper, slipping the dress back on with shaky hands. "I don't have time."

There isn't a mirror to check my reflection, but I'm positive I'm a mess. Tate and I took a bath at one point in the night. But before we had time to wash anything, like my face, I was bent over the side of the tub and getting railed from behind.

My stomach clenches at the memory, and I can't help but smile. *Was there a surface in this suite that I didn't get pounded on last night?*

I ignore the temptation to climb back in bed for one final hoorah and instead grab my purse and the rose Tate brought to me at Ruma. I start to leave but stop.

My breaths are hurried, and my heart pounds. *What do I do? Do I walk out without a goodbye of any sort?*

That seems like a viable solution, and one that's merited. I told him this was a one-night thing. He must expect that I'll be gone ... *right?*

I groan, finding a small pad of paper and a pen on the desk by the wall.

*Thanks for an incredible night.*

"How do I sign this?" I whisper, nibbling my bottom lip.

I can't put Aurora, and writing Kelly is more than I can handle this morning. After the way he treated me yesterday—so sweet and kind—my guilt is exceedingly high about using a fake name. Acid bubbles up my throat at the thought.

"Just ... *put something*," I whisper, scribbling a final line.

*Call me. Xo*

I roll my eyes, realizing how ridiculous that sentiment is—considering he doesn't know my name or my phone number—and toss the pen next to the paper.

On an exhale, I turn to leave and spot the blueberry pie on the couch. My stomach growls.

I glance at the bedroom door again before grabbing the pie. After carrying it to the small kitchenette, I locate a paper plate and a plastic knife. My handiwork looks more like a serial killer than a chef, but one slice finds its way to the plate. I carry it across the room and leave it with the note.

A sound makes me jump. I cover my mouth, listening closely,

uncertain where it came from. I watch the bedroom door, praying it doesn't open.

*I have to get out of here before it gets weird.*

With my purse and rose in one hand, and the rest of the pie in the other, I slip into the hallway.

The elevator is only a few steps away. I hit the down button and shift my weight from foot to foot. Finally, after what feels like an eternity, it opens.

Luckily, the elevator is empty, and I hit the button for the lobby.

"Oh God!" My jaw drops as I catch a look at myself in the mirrors lining the car. "I look like a tiger has mauled me."

I set my things on the floor and try to make my hair somewhat presentable. Nothing can be done about the raccoon eyes from the mascara, and my lips are swollen from Tate's onslaught. All I can do is hope people think it's filler.

My phone begins to ring. *Dammit.* "Where are you?" I groan as I forage to the bottom of my purse, barely answering it before the elevator's doors open.

"Hello?" I ask, sweeping my possessions into my arms without making eye contact at the couple waiting to board.

"Why do you sound … rushed?" Jamie asks.

"Because I am." I tuck my chin and step into the hallway. "This is not a good time. Can I call you back?"

"No. Now I'm curious. What are you doing?"

I fake a smile at one of the ladies at the front desk as I scurry past to my bank of elevators.

"You probably won't believe me even if I tell you," I say.

"Try me."

I sigh, hitting the up arrow to go to my room. Thankfully, it's too early for much traffic because the elevator is waiting and empty.

"Are you still there?" she asks.

Once the doors close, I sag against the wall. "I did what you suggested."

I drop the line in the air, the weight of it similar to a dumbbell dropped from a bridge into the sea. I can almost hear my admission sinking into Jamie's brain.

"You had a—"

"Yes. I met him on the plane," I say, talking fast. "He was young, insanely hot, and charmed my dress right off me."

*"Holy shit, Ror."*

*If you only knew.* "I can't get into it right now. I'm almost late for my conference because not only did I get fucked until about four o'clock this morning, I fell asleep in his room, and now I'm doing a walk of shame through the hotel with no bra or panties, trying to get to my room so I can get cleaned up, dressed, and down to the conference room before I miss the keynote speech." I suck in a hasty breath. "And I stole his pie."

"Is that a euphemism?"

"A what?" I make a face. "No. I actually stole an entire blueberry pie. I did leave him a piece for breakfast, but that isn't the point. Don't get hung up on that."

"I am so proud of you," she says, laughing.

"This is not good, Jamie! I just had the best sex of my life, and I gave the guy a fake name," I say, lowering my voice as I step off onto my floor.

"Why would you do that?"

"Because ..." I dig around in my purse again for my key card. "Because I didn't expect all of this to happen. I was trying to be safe and thought an air of anonymity would be fun. I don't know. I'm not good at this."

"Clearly."

I march into my room and toss the pie, purse, and rose onto the bed. Then I plop down next to it.

My brain is spinning too fast to sort through all the jumbled thoughts. But there's one I can pluck out. A very important one.

*Tate.*

Memories from last night float through my mind. I can feel Tate's hands on me, both aggressive and tender. His smile warms my heart and makes my knees weak. The way he looked at me has me sitting taller. I've never felt more beautiful, sexier, or more desirable than I do this morning even though I currently *look* like a hag.

I'll never forget a single detail of last night. I'll probably never lose the dull ache of wanting him, either. Still, it was worth it.

I stare at the dark television and smile. "I don't regret it."

"I'm glad."

"I was afraid I would," I admit. "Maybe I didn't play it off perfectly, and I'm not sure I'd do a fake name again because something about lying is driving me crazy. But this single encounter has split me open—in more ways than one."

"Girl! That's what I'm talking about."

I laugh. "It was so good, Jamie. I've been fucked in ways I didn't know were possible. At one point, I was lying on the edge of the bed, right? He lifted my legs and pulled me up and to him. I was basically lying with the top of my head on the mattress and my legs over his shoulders. I don't know what kind of magic that was, but yeah, he was hitting my G-spot and playing with my clit at the same time while making eye contact …"

My thighs are soaked once again. *I'm going to have to masturbate before I can leave this room.*

"Can we talk about this later?" I ask. "I have a little more than an hour to get ready, and you should see me right now."

"If you don't call me as soon as you're done today, I will catch a flight there. I mean it. I want every single detail."

I smile. "I'll give them to you. Promise. But I really do need to go."

"I have a client walking in the door right now, anyway. Love you. Drink your water."

"Love you, too. Bye."

"Bye." I exhale harshly and check my phone. "Shit!"

There are three missed calls from my boss, and one voicemail. I spring to my feet and hit play.

"Hey, Aurora, it's Charlie. I'm sorry to call you so late on a Friday night, but I need to talk to you as soon as you can give me a call back. Okay? Thanks. Call my cell, please."

Blood pounds in my temples as I clear my throat. Then I hit Charlie's name.

"Aurora, hi. Good morning," he says almost instantly.

The sound of his voice piques my curiosity. It's flatter than usual. Deeper. It's without his usual addictive excitement and energy.

"Good morning," I say, kicking off my heels. "I'm sorry I missed your calls."

"It's no problem. But thank you for calling me this morning."

"Of course. I called you back as soon as I got your voicemail."

He sighs. "I hate to ask this of you, but I don't see another way." He pauses, giving me enough time to full-out panic. "Is there any way you can return to Nashville today?"

*What?* "I'm flying back this evening after the conference."

"I was hoping you could miss the conference and come back as early as you can this afternoon." He blows out a heavy breath—the kind that someone holds when they're about to break. "Aurora, my mother is in hospice."

My heart drops. "Oh, Charlie. I'm so sorry."

"Me, too. It all happened very suddenly. She had pneumonia last week, and we didn't think it was that big of a deal. My sister called me a few days ago and told me that Mom has taken a turn for the worse. She's in her eighties, and I knew her health was starting to deteriorate, so I informed management that I'd probably need to leave soon. But last night, my sister called and said hospice had been called, and I need to get back to Salt Lake City immediately."

I sit again, tears gathering in my eyes. "I lost my parents a few years ago. I really am sorry. If you need anything—even an ear to listen—I'm here for you. Please know that."

"I truly appreciate it. And I might take you up on that."

"The offer stands indefinitely."

"I'm leaving Nashville tomorrow afternoon," he says. "I have no idea if or when I'll return. But I need to pass the baton to someone, at least for the time being, and you're the person most informed of our plans for the rebrand."

"Okay."

"So I'd really appreciate it if you could come back to the office—today, if at all possible—and let me go over a bunch of things with you."

I swallow past a lump in my throat. "Yes, of course. Whatever you need."

"I'm sorry to do this to you."

"Don't be sorry. Are you kidding me? I'm at this conference to help you, but if I'm more helpful to you there, then that's where I'll be."

"You are the best, Aurora. I hope you know that."

His words make me smile. "Thank you. You've been an excellent boss."

"Thanks."

I look around the room. "Let me get my things together and find a flight. I'll text you my ETA as soon as I have it."

"See you soon."

"See you soon. Goodbye, Charlie."

"Goodbye."

I waste no time pulling up flight information and find a flight leaving in three hours. I get it booked, cancel my original ticket, and find Charlie's name in my texts.

> Me: I should be in the office by two thirty or three. I'll keep you posted.

I take a breath, toss my phone on the bed, and head to the shower to wash off the most amazing night of my life.

*First class has nothing on you, Columbus.*

But now, it's back to the real world.

## Chapter Ten

Tate

"Ugh," I groan, patting around on the bedside table for my phone.

My hand smacks an empty water bottle, sending it flying to the floor, before I finally locate my irritating device. I raise my head high enough to see the screen and click *end* on the alarm. *Thank God.*

"There are few things I hate more than alarms," I say, smiling as I roll over to pull Kelly against me again. "But I guess we should—Kelly?"

The sheets are pulled back, and the pillow is still dented from her head, but she's gone.

"Kelly?"

I sit up, wide awake. I listen closely for the sound of running water or her voice from the living room. Crickets.

*Maybe she's in the bath again.* My lips twitch. *Or maybe she couldn't resist that blueberry pie any longer.*

*The Situation*

I yank the sheets off my body and get to my feet.

"Hey, Kel? Where are you?"

My stomach tightens as I peer into the bathroom. It's just how we left it last night. The tub is half filled with water. Towels are on the floor. My Dopp kit is halfway under the vanity because I swept it off the counter so Aurora could sit in its place. It was the perfect height for me to cage her in and worship her body.

Long, leisurely kisses. Sucking those perfect, heavy tits. Running my hands over rounded hips and stomach. Her body moved beneath my hands, and her little moans and whispers were so damn hot.

*God, that's one fantastic memory.*

I grab my hardening cock and make my way into the living room.

"Kelly?" I might be late to the conference, but I can't leave this room without fucking her one more time. "Where are you, gorgeous?"

I round the corner. Then come to a full stop.

"What the hell?"

My heartbeat quickens as I scan the room.

Her dress is gone. I don't see her heels.

"What's going on?" I ask the empty room.

I wander through it like a lost little boy, looking for any sign of her.

My brain races through last night. The last thing I remember is her curling up next to me with her head on my chest and falling asleep.

*Did I say something wrong? Did I push her too far? Did I make her uncomfortable?*

I force a swallow, running a hand over my head.

"She couldn't have just left me."

I make a face, so fucking confused, but just as I pass the desk, I notice a slice of pie on a paper plate. I glance over my shoulder to see the pie box is gone, too.

The hotel-embossed notepad is beside the pie.

*Thanks for an incredible night.*
*Call me. Xo*

I jerk the notepad off the desk and read it again. "No fucking way."

The room is eerily quiet as I contemplate this peculiar situation. *She left me?* This has never happened before. I usually have to invent a meeting or an obligation to get women to leave.

*And Kelly left me?*

"This is bullshit," I say, picking up the phone and calling the front desk.

"Good morning, Mr. Brewer. This is Connie. How may I be of service?"

"Good morning, Connie. I had a guest in my room last night who is also staying here. Can you tell me what room Kelly Kapowski is in?"

"I'm sorry, Mr. Brewer. I can't give out that information."

I scan the room again. My sights land on a lacy black bra peeking out from under the sofa.

"I understand," I say, picking up Kelly's bra. It dangles off my fingertips. "But she left something ... *personal* in my room. She might be looking for it later."

"That's unfortunate. Would you like me to send someone up to get it? We can put it in our Lost and Found."

*Not a chance.*

"I think I better keep this in my possession, Connie."

"As you wish. I'm happy to put a note in there that you have one of her items, if you'd like?"

"You know what? I would like that. Thank you."

"Of course. Is there anything else I can do for you?"

*Yeah, give me her room number.* "That's it. Thank you again."

"You're welcome. Enjoy your stay at Picante. Goodbye."

*The Situation*

"Goodbye."

I replace the receiver, then mosey around the room.

She must have forgotten to include her phone number in the note. That's the only explanation that makes sense. She had a meeting this morning, too. Maybe it started earlier than mine, and she didn't want to wake me.

It has to be that.

I bring her bra to my nose and breathe it in. My cock twitches immediately at the memory of her. It's sweet and feminine, just like her.

I'll never smell vanilla again and not get a hard-on.

The suite feels too big. Too empty. Too quiet. There's too much space for me to let my mind run wild.

Surely, she didn't leave because she isn't into me ... *right?*

"Nah," I say, heading back into the bedroom. "Her note said it was an incredible night, and I should call her. She just forgot to leave her number."

I'll just find her on Social.

I grab my phone and pull up the app. Then I type in *Kelly Kapowski*.

Four accounts pull up with the same chick that is definitely not my Kelly.

"The fuck?"

I open a browser and search for her there.

"Why is this only pulling up a television show?" I open one article and discover that Kelly Kapowski is the name of a character from a teenage sitcom. "Her mom must've been a fan. People are so weird."

The knot in my stomach grows tighter by the minute. I can't shake it off. I'm sure it's just a case of confusion, disappointment, and blue balls. Still, I need someone to tell me that I'm overreacting.

I grab my phone and call Carys.

"Why are you calling me so early on a Saturday morning?" Carys asks, yawning.

"Hello to you, too."

"Is anyone dying?" Gannon asks from the background.

"No," I say. "Why would you ask me that?"

"Then why the hell are you calling us this early?" Gannon asks.

I roll my eyes. "I'm not calling you. I'm calling Carys."

"You're going to learn boundaries one way or the other," my brother says.

"Yeah. Later," I say. "Carys, I'm having a slight emergency, and I need your help."

"For the love of God, Tate ..." Gannon mutters, sighing heavily for my benefit, I'm sure.

The line gets fuzzy for a moment before Carys's voice rings through the line.

"What's your emergency?" she asks.

"He probably found out Kelly isn't real," Gannon says.

"She is real, asshole. Trust me. I fucked her for six or seven hours last night."

Carys sighs. "So ... emergency?" Carys asks impatiently.

"She might be real, but she was gone this morning," I say, the words a little wobbly as they come out.

"What do you mean she was gone this morning?" Carys asks.

I pace the room. "I don't know. She was gone. I went to sleep with her on top of me, and I woke up alone. She took her clothes and the pie and left."

"Pie?" Carys asks.

"Tate, are you drunk?" Gannon asks.

"No, I'm not drunk, asshole. God, I hate you sometimes."

"We have something in common after all." Gannon snorts. "I hate to be the one to tell you this. Actually, I'm not. I'm overjoyed that I get to be the one who tells you this—Kelly isn't real. At worst, you have a drug problem we don't know about, and you imagined all of this. At best, she gave you a fake name."

I gasp. "Kelly would never do that."

"You sure?"

*Hell, yes, I'm sure ... aren't I?*

My gut tenses even harder. It almost feels like I've taken a punch from Ripley because the wind has been knocked out of me. *How dare he suggest something so asinine?*

"We had a connection," I say, talking over Gannon's chuckles. "I was charming. I took my clothes off. I entertained her with stories and oysters, and I made her come—"

"Stop!" Carys groans. "We get the picture."

"I'm starting to worry she got sick or something," I say.

"Or maybe she just played you," Gannon says with entirely too much glee.

I narrow my eyes. "She didn't play me. She was totally into me." I start pacing again. "But let's play devil's advocate for a minute and say there was a chance she wasn't into me. How would you even substantiate that idea? I'm Tate fucking Brewer. Women love me."

"All of them but her," Gannon says.

"You don't know what you're talking about."

"No, you're right. I don't. I've never had a woman walk out on me —*ouch*! I'm kidding, Carys. I'm kidding."

"No, you're not," she says. "No one in their right mind would walk out on you. I just don't want to think about you with other women."

"There were no women before you. You're the only one who mattered."

"Come on," I groan. "Let's focus on me here."

The sound of them kissing crackles through the phone.

"I need a new best friend," I say.

"Yes, you do," Gannon says, although the sound is broken up by what I'm assuming is Carys's lips.

"I really should've fucked your stepmommy," I tell Carys. "Then you could've known what it's like to have someone from your family reject you."

Carys laughs. "Aurora isn't my stepmommy anymore, remember?

So if you had hooked up with her, she wouldn't have been my family. Besides, I like Aurora. She wouldn't reject me."

"Like Kelly rejected you." Gannon chuckles again.

"I hate you," I say. "Both of you. All I needed was for you to tell me that there must've been an emergency, and that Kelly will call me later."

"We aren't lying to you," Gannon says.

*This bastard.*

"Tate, I'm sure she'll get ahold of you," Carys says. "Have you ever known a woman not to call?"

I grin. "No."

"And have you ever wanted a woman you couldn't get?" she asks.

My grin turns smug, and I stand taller. "Absolutely not."

"So she probably had work this morning or something and had to run. She clearly knows what room you're in, and I'm sure she'll be knocking by dinnertime."

"See? That's all I needed." I move to the bathroom and flip on the shower. "Was it that hard?"

"Oh, it's *very* hard right now," Carys says, whimpering.

I roll my eyes again. "Bye."

Carys yelps and giggles as the call is disconnected on her end.

I don't have time to put my phone down before it starts pinging. I glance down to see my text app going off repeatedly.

> Ripley: Well, well, well. 😼

> Bianca: Be nice, Ripley.

> Ripley: I am being nice.

> Jason: I'd like to think I'm too mature for this, but I'm up with my coffee in hand.

> Renn: Gannon works fast.

*The Situation*

*That fucker.*

I know this is about me without asking. I'm partially impressed that Gannon has lowered himself enough to gossip. Maybe he's human, after all. But I'm mostly irritated in their amusement at my predicament.

> Ripley: Gannon works fast, but Kelly runs faster.
>
> Renn: 🙄
>
> Jason: Yikes.
>
> Bianca: Oh, lord.
>
> Me: What did I ever do to you?
>
> Ripley: I think Kelly is asking herself the same question this morning—what did Tate do to me?

I reach into the shower and turn the water off.

Me: She had to work this morning. It's no big deal.

Bianca: I believe you.

Jason: I don't.

Me: You know what *I* don't believe? I don't believe I had to fly commercial to Columbus. That's what I don't believe.

Renn: But if you'd have flown Brewer Air, you wouldn't have met your fake girlfriend.

Me: SHE IS NOT FAKE. 😬

Ripley: Her name was.

Jason: Have you thought about looking her up online?

Ripley: 🙈

I stare at the phone. *Yes, motherfucker, I did. And it wasn't helpful.*

Me: You guys are wrong. You don't know her like I do. We shared something special. We had a connection.

Ripley: Suuuuuure.

Me: Your jealousy is getting ugly, Rip.

Ripley: Please.

Me: I'm not dog sitting Pancake and Waffles anymore.

Ripley: Yes, you will.

*The Situation*

I will. He's right. I love those damn dogs. But I'm not telling him that.

I glance at the clock.

> Me: I don't have time for this. I have to get ready for work because some of us don't get to stay home all weekend and enjoy ourselves.

> Gannon: I'm quite enjoying myself right now.

*I'm going to kill him.*

I close out of the app and don't look at it again.

Instead, I jump into the shower and try to figure out how to get ahold of Kelly Kapowski.

## Chapter Eleven

# Aurora

"Good morning," Tally whispers from my office doorway.

I look up and return her hesitant smile. Her brows pull together as she takes me in, undoubtedly noticing my frazzled state. *Is it bedtime yet?* Running on five hours' sleep over the past three days will do that to a person.

"Are you okay?" she asks.

"Come in and close the door behind you."

"What's going on?" She takes a seat across from me. "With all due respect, you look ... not your best."

"Gee, thanks."

She grimaces, and I smile.

"I'm joking." I sigh. "It's been a long weekend, and I'm exhausted."

"How did the conference go?"

## The Situation

I shrug. "I don't know. I wasn't there."

She flashes me a look like I've lost my mind.

"We have a meeting in an hour, and you're going to hear it then. So I might as well tell you now," I say. "Charlie is gone."

"Charlie is dead? *Oh my God.*"

"No," I say, shaking my head. "No, he's not dead. But he has left the company."

Her eyes widen. "Why?"

"He called me ... well, he called me on Friday, but I didn't get his messages until Saturday. Basically, his mother was put into hospice, and he needed to be home with his family."

"Oh, man. I hate that for him. Is he okay?"

My heart tugs in my chest. "I think he's as okay as anyone can be when you find out that your parent is passing away."

A wave of despair breaks over me as I recall the moment that I found out both of my parents had been in a terrible accident, and that my father had passed, and my mother was on life support. A ball of fire settles into the base of my throat. For a few seconds, it's hard to breathe.

"Wow," she says on an exhale. She stares out my office window as if she's trying to process it all.

I glance at the legal pad full of notes I took on Saturday evening with Charlie. He insisted on sharing every file, note, and inspiration he had for the Raptors rebrand. I'm awed by his marketing prowess and vision. I also wish I'd had more time to learn from him. For someone leaving a company, especially under such dire circumstances, he was certainly upstanding in how much time he spent preparing his assistant.

I'm convinced, however, that more than anything, he was keeping himself busy until his flight took off on Sunday morning. Preoccupying oneself is something I can relate to these days.

Tally sighs. "Not to be insensitive, but what do we do now? Are they replacing him? Are we just waiting around until he comes back?"

"I honestly don't know. I assume that's what we'll discuss in the meeting this morning."

"So I'm guessing you flew back from Columbus on Saturday?"

I nod. "I came here straight from the airport Saturday afternoon. We were here until nine o'clock that night, just going over things and ..." I frown. "I don't think he wanted to be home alone with his thoughts. And since I've lost both of my parents, I was a good sounding board."

"Was that hard for you? I mean, I can imagine that it would be difficult to talk about losing your mom and dad, especially when someone else is in the heavy emotional stages of it."

"I don't think anyone ever enjoys talking about things like that. But I guess I feel like if I can use my grief and pain to make someone else feel more seen or heard, then at least it's doing some good."

Tally smiles at me, nodding. "I love you."

Her declaration makes me laugh.

"I mean it," she says, laughing too. "You are the best person. You're kind to everyone. Thoughtful. You're so full of wisdom."

"Okay. Easy there. Now I know you're just flattering me."

"I am not." Her laughter fades. "I feel fortunate that I've gotten to work with you."

My cheeks flush as I grab my coffee. "Well, I feel fortunate to have my very own hype woman."

"Hey, speaking of hype women, weren't you a professional cheerleader?"

I nod. "I cheered for the Illinois Legends, the pro football team, in my twenties."

"See? You're the epitome of cool. I've learned so much about not only marketing from you but also how to be a strong woman."

I don't know what to say to that because I certainly don't feel like a strong woman all the time or most of the time. In fact, if Tally had met me when I was reeling from learning I'd married a selfish, egotistical bastard, she might have different thoughts about me. *The way he treated his daughter was disgusting.* But it does make me feel good to know that I might be having a positive impact on my intern.

She shifts in her seat. "On that note, I might not be able to help Charlie, but I can help you. What can I do to assist you, Aurora?"

I look around my desk and search for an answer.

I've fixated on this job for the past day and a half. I've been over every aspect of things front to back, side to side. I promised Charlie that I would maintain our vision, and I intend to do just that. But I've focused on it for so long that I need a break to refresh my brain.

"Thank you for asking," I say. "I'm sure there will be a million things you can do to help. But for right now, I want to mentally check out for a few minutes while I can."

"Understandable."

I lean against my desktop. "Why don't you tell me about your weekend? How was pickleball?"

"Well, let's just say I'm not only a legend on the court but I'm one off the court, as well."

"I expected no less."

She laughs, settling into her seat. "It turns out that I'm one heck of a pickleball teacher. I took my boyfriend from a four to a seven in just a couple of days. Pickleball doesn't come quite as naturally to him as it does to me. But I've put together a good practice schedule for him while I'm out of town, and I'll go home as much as I can over the next couple of months. We'll be ready to kick butt by the time the tournament rolls around."

"This fascinates me."

"Why?"

"I don't know. I guess I didn't know people took pickleball this seriously."

"Girl, people talk about this tournament all damn year. In the middle of our town square is a statue of a pickle holding a ball. Corny, but also cute. Anyway, there are little plaques around the bottom of the statue with the names of the tourney champs from every year going back to the 1970s." She winks. "My name is there multiple times."

"I'm glad you had a good weekend."

She smiles. "I did. It was also just nice to see my boyfriend. We're doing this long-distance thing that I didn't think would work, but we've been making it happen. It's hard, for sure ..." Her smile turns ornery. "But that only makes it harder, if you know what I mean."

"Yeah, I know what you mean."

I can't think about that right now. I pluck my brain out of the trenches before it can fully create a picture by joining *Tate* and *hard*.

I'm at work. I'm not being paid to fantasize.

"Speaking of that, do you have anything to share with me, boss lady?"

The twinkle in her eye makes me grin.

"You're probably thinking that now isn't the right time," she says.

"Or ever."

"You opened the door to this when we spoke on Friday. So naturally, I'll be thinking about what might've happened with you, and you'll wonder if you'll wind up telling me. You might as well get it out of the way so we can attend this meeting in a few minutes and focus. As my boss, you should clear the air so we can be productive."

I laugh at the perfectly satisfied look on her face.

"You're only laughing because you know I'm right," she says, grinning.

I settle back in my seat and try to decide how to handle this with Tally. In a perfect world, I wouldn't have brought this up with her. But I did, and now it only makes sense that she wants a resolution to the issue.

*What a resolution it was.* I stifle a moan.

Although I've been focused on work for the past couple of days, Tate has definitely been on my mind. Every time I think of him, a warmth floods my body, and a smile splits my cheeks. Being with him was exactly what I wanted and exactly what I needed. No one ever gets both of those things at once.

I've wondered what he got out of our night together. Despite his words of praise, I'm sure he's on to his next hookup. *As he should.*

But *I'm* a different woman than the one I was when I boarded the plane on Friday. That version of me was hopeful but scared to hope too much. I was quietly fearful that the best years of my life had passed me by, and I'd made peace with the possibility that I might wind up alone for the rest of my life.

But that was the me then. *This me?* I have a whole new perspective.

One night with Tate was all it took to realize that I haven't really lived. I've settled for far less than I deserve. I've been accepting of things that didn't suit me, benefit me, or were for me.

I've been content with living my life in mediocrity so that other people can be comfortable.

It's a stunning revelation.

It took a stranger to show me what I've been missing. A man I don't even know showed me more passion than my two husbands who took an oath before God to love, honor, and cherish me. It's wild.

"So ..." Tally prompts, watching me expectantly. "Don't sit there and pretend you don't have a story for me because I can see it in your eyes."

I take a deep breath. "Fine. I'm not giving you a ton of details because you are my intern, and we do need to keep this professional."

"I get it. But also, you do realize that if I weren't your intern, we'd totally be hanging out, right?"

"Tally, I could be your mother."

"The coolest mother ever." She points at me. "Don't get sidetracked. Spill it."

"Fine." A bubble of excitement stirs in my stomach. "Yes, I did see Tate on Friday."

She fist-pumps the air.

"I went down to the restaurant for dinner, and he happened to be there waiting for me."

"Seriously?"

"With a rose," I say, grinning.

She dances in her seat.

"And he'd made reservations for us."

"A man with a plan. We love it."

*Yes, we do.* "And we might've gone back to his room after."

"Aurora, you little minx!"

My face turns red. "And that's all you're getting."

"That wasn't all he was getting, it seems."

"Stop it." I laugh. "Seriously. I've overshared as it is."

She scoots to the edge of the chair. "I have one question, and then I'll let it go."

I stare at her.

"Did you at least give him your real name?" she asks.

I shake my head. "A part of me feels guilty for lying to him about it. But when it comes down to it, I'm glad I didn't."

"You can't get an encore if he doesn't know who you are!"

"Exactly."

She holds her head in her hands like her mind is blown.

I could explain it to her. I could tell her that I can't get in too deep with the first man I meet after my divorce. And I certainly can't let myself fall for a man who's probably cool with never seeing me again.

He got what he wanted. I did, too. And what happened in Ohio needs to stay there.

"Okay," I say, organizing papers in front of me. "We have a meeting in about half an hour. I have no idea who's going to be there or what they're going to say. I just need us to be as prepared as we can be for whatever comes our way. Charlie is counting on us, and I gave him my word."

The playfulness of a few moments ago is gone, and Tally's in work mode.

"In that case, I need to run to my desk and make sure I'm organized," she says, getting to her feet.

"Great."

"Don't worry, Aurora. We're going to dazzle them with our abilities," she says, a nod punctuating her statement. "By the sound of it, it'll be the second time you've dazzled someone this week."

"Tally …"

She heads for the door. "I'm kidding. I won't bring it up again, but I couldn't let that opportunity pass."

"Meet me in the conference room at nine fifty."

"I'll be there."

She closes the door behind her.

I sit back in my chair and grab my coffee, letting the heat of the mug warm my hands. For the first time since the start of the weekend, I'm able to catch my breath. I can think clearly, too.

Tate's smile pops up in my brain.

Well, kind of clearly …

## Chapter Twelve

# Tate

"That's a no."

I deny Gannon's call and pull out of my neighborhood.

The Monday morning sun is bright and warm. It should be enough to lift my spirits. Even if I wake up in a bad mood, the sun has a way of straightening me out before I get to the office.

*Usually.*

I have a feeling that won't work today.

Gannon calls again. I deny him for a second time.

I kept my eyes open for Kelly all day on Saturday. That night, I sat at the bar in Ruma for far too long in hopes that she'd come down for dinner. I watched for her at the airport on Sunday and spent my time sitting in the traveler's lounge searching for her online.

Social media platforms. Search engines. I looked everywhere I could think of ... and came up empty-handed.

## The Situation

The only Kelly Kapowski who came up for me was a fictional character.

Another call from my eldest brother. I send him to voicemail just as fast as I did the first two times.

This thing with Kelly is bizarre. I don't understand it. She wrote *call me* on the note she left behind. But how do I call her with no number?

It must be an unfortunate omission or misunderstanding. That's all. Or maybe her name is Kellyanne or Keely, and everyone calls her Kelly.

*Yeah. It has to be something like that. What else could it be?*

If I were a lesser man, I might entertain the idea that the name was made up so that I couldn't find her. If I were anyone else—Gannon, for example—I'd expect that she probably played me or used me for my dick. Guys like that get taken advantage of all the time.

But I'm me. That's not the case. I'm a catch.

I downshift and slide into the middle lane to pass a car piddling around in the fast lane.

My phone rings yet again, and I start to decline it. But just before I do, I notice the number is Carys's and not Gannon's.

My stomach tenses. *What if something's wrong? What if something happened to Ivy?*

Shit.

"Hey," I say, my brows pulled together.

"Answer your fucking phone," my brother says.

*Asshole.*

"I called you three times," he says.

"And I sent you to voicemail three times. It would've been four had I realized this was you, too."

He groans. "Why are you acting like a child?"

"I'm not. I'm acting like a man who doesn't want to hear your bullshit before I've had lunch." I get back into the fast lane. "Actually, I don't want to hear your bullshit at any point today. Let me stand corrected."

"You don't want to hear my bullshit? *Aw.* Is Tate feeling like a big boy today?"

"Fuck off."

Gannon chuckles. "Don't be pissed at me because you got played this weekend."

*I should've just turned my phone off this morning.*

I re-grip the steering wheel and squeeze, counting to ten before I say a bunch of shit I don't mean. Sure, Gannon is being a dick, but he's also messing with me because that's what brothers do. At least we have a relationship these days where he feels comfortable enough to joke around with me.

That wasn't always the case.

Under normal circumstances, I'd crack a joke or make fun of him, but I'm a little on edge today. I'd probably push it too far.

"I'm assuming you want something since you called a million times," I say, zipping past a line of cars.

"I need a favor."

"Awesome. Call someone who cares."

"Cut the shit, Tate. Carys woke up sicker than hell, and Ivy has a fever this morning, too. I'm staying home to take care of my girls."

*Oh no.* "Are they okay? Do you guys need anything?"

"I have a call into the doctor's office now. I suspect it's a virus, but I'm having someone come by the house to check it out. Can't risk it."

He takes a deep breath that raises my hackles.

Gannon doesn't ask too much from me on a personal level. Ripley calls with favors. Renn calls with manipulations. *Come over for dinner, and let's build this coffee table while you're here.* Jason doesn't ask for jack shit.

I give Gannon a ton of hell for "making me" travel for work. While I do hate it and want to segue into a different position, he's not punishing me or giving me the short end of the stick. Schmoozing people is what I'm good at. It's a space where I've been valuable to the family business. But the truth of the matter is that Gannon is fair and an excellent leader at Brewer Group. Under his leadership, we'll soar heads and tails higher than our father would've ever managed. But he never asks for help on a personal level.

If he's requesting my assistance as his brother—if it's to benefit his wife and baby girl, I'm in. And the bastard knows it.

"What do you need from me?" I ask, rolling my eyes.

"I need you to sit in on a meeting at the Raptors offices."

*That's the last place I want to be.* I groan.

"Look, I'm not any happier about this than you are," he says. "But that doesn't change the fact that the Raptors administration is in limbo once again, and someone from our family needs to be there as a show of support. As a sign of strength and continuity."

"Is McCabe coming back?"

"Honestly, I'm not sure. I'm looking for an interim marketing director until he does, or we find someone to replace him."

I blow out a breath, turn on my signal, and cut across two lanes of traffic to hit the exit for the hockey offices.

"What time is this meeting?" I ask, resolved to my fate.

"It's at ten."

I glance at the clock. "You mean in twenty minutes?"

"Yeah, I know it's inconvenient. I thought it was at one. I fucked up."

*Nice of you to admit that.* "You're lucky I'm close. I had two virtual meetings this morning from home, and was on my way to the office, so the Raptors office is close by."

"I appreciate this. And, so you know, I told human resources to start looking for someone to take a load off your plate."

I flinch, and my tires hit the rumble strips on the right side of the road.

"What's that sound?" Gannon asks.

"I almost wrecked. Did you say you're going to hire someone to help me? For real?"

He sighs dramatically. "I have to do something. You won't stop complaining."

"Do you have a fever, too?"

"I could change my mind, you know."

"Let's not make any rash decisions," I say, pulling into the Raptors parking lot. I find the spot with a sign reading *Brewer* and park my Mercedes SL600. "I'm here. Anything I should know about this?"

I cut the engine, grab my keys, and climb out of the car. The lights flash as I lock it behind me.

"Not really," he says. "You're just there to show we're involved in the business. We've been making great headway, and McCabe assured me that he's met with his assistant and ensured she's up to date with his plans. We just need a Brewer representative in a chair."

I buzz myself in and nod at the security guard on my way to the elevator bank.

"I still think we try to sell this team," I say softly, stepping into an empty elevator car to whisk me to the top floor.

"That would be amazing, but we can't sell it as it stands. The revenue is shit. The forecast is dismal. And I refuse to take a loss on it. It would be like Dad got us one last time."

I bite my tongue.

The topic of our father is much more sensitive with Gannon than it is with me. As the oldest son, Gannon's relationship with Dad was arguably the most complicated. He was beyond devastated when Dad showed his true colors and has had the hardest time accepting it, I think. But we've all dealt with it in our own way. I, for one, always thought he was an arrogant son of a bitch, and whether it's the correct response or not, I frankly enjoy the thought of him sitting behind bars for the rest of his life while we're on the outside living ours.

My only regret is that Renn's wife, Blakely, and Bianca had to shoulder their unfair share of his insanity. I could strangle him with my bare hands for that.

"I get it," I say instead, stepping out onto the executive level. "We'll get this turned around. But I need to go figure out where this meeting is being held. I'll keep you posted."

*The Situation*

"Thanks, Tate."

"You're welcome. Tell Carys that I hope she feels better. Give Ivy kisses from her favorite uncle."

"Done. I told her this morning that her favorite uncle Ripley was worried."

I gasp. "Look, there are lines that shouldn't be crossed ..."

He chuckles. "Bye."

"Goodbye," I say, grinning as I end the call.

I slide my phone into my pocket and pause at the reception desk to say hello. The pretty redhead who must be new to the facility directs me to the conference room in question, and I make my way down the corridor.

Thanks to Carys's incessant chatter about plants and the way she leaves little potted ones in every space she touches, I notice that a few green things might brighten the place. It's very dull and cold here. Or maybe that's on brand for hockey. *What the hell do I know?*

My footsteps slow, and a smile curls my lips.

*Kelly loves design. What would she do with this?*

I sigh, frustration licking at my nerves. I have to stop thinking about her—at least while I'm working. I keep thinking she'll fade from my memory. But it's been days since I saw her, and she still takes up most of the real estate in my brain.

I wish I could figure out why.

Sure, I'm wildly attracted to her in every way. Her brain, body, and intelligence are the ultimate package. It probably doesn't hurt that she left without saying goodbye. That leaves me with no closure. I've used that trick on women a time or two. It keeps them wanting more. But it's more than that. Dare I say it's deeper?

It sounds crazy to think I'm this into a woman I've spent one night with, but I can't get her out of my head.

"Mr. Brewer, hi. Good morning," Daniel Garrey says as he exits his office. He extends his hand, and we shake as we make our way down the hall. "It's good to see you."

"It's good to see you too, Dan. How are things?"

"They're very good. I'm more optimistic and pleased with the progress that we've made in the past few months than I have in the seven years I've worked for the Raptors. Things are looking up."

"That's great to hear."

"I know we lost McCabe, and that's a big loss," he says. "But I have a lot of confidence in his vision and his staff. Have you met them before?"

I shake my head.

"You'll love them. They're smart and understand how to reach people in today's world. McCabe played a significant role in changing the culture around here. Aurora and Tally will keep leading the charge, I'm sure."

My phone buzzes, and I pull it out of my pocket. I see a text from Jason.

"I'll meet you down there," I say to Dan.

He nods and rounds the corner.

> Jason: I want to apologize for the aircraft issue on Friday.

> Me: Appreciate that.

> Jason: We have a couple of planes down for maintenance right now, so if you can get your travel schedules to my assistant as early as possible, I'll make sure we can accommodate you.

*Why can't Gannon be this easy to deal with?*

*The Situation*

> Me: Great. Thanks so much.
>
> Jason: I'll see you Wednesday?
>
> Me: As long as Mimi doesn't cancel on me. 😊
>
> Jason: Yeah, right. 🙄 See you then.
>
> Me: Later.

I lock my screen and turn the corner. A few people are chatting away as they exit the conference room. Another group waits near the doors for the room to empty.

I straighten my tie, thinking through my impromptu welcome speech I'll undoubtedly be expected to give, when my gaze is plucked out of the air by a pair of intimately familiar dark eyes.

My feet falter.

I flinch, my brows pulling together in confusion just before they rise in surprise.

*Holy shit.*

"Kelly?" I ask incredulously. *What's she doing here?*

I blink a few times to see if I'm hallucinating.

*Nope. She's still there.*

Kelly is somehow more beautiful than I remember. Her hair is pulled back into a neat knot on top of her head. Long, light gray pants make her legs appear a mile long. A soft pink top is a stark contrast to her tanned skin. All I can think about is how her cheeks flush that same color as she's coming on my cock.

"Aurora, Tally," Dan says, holding the door open. "After you, ladies."

Kelly's eyes grow wide, and those full lips that feel like pillows wrapped around me are pursed together in shock.

"Kelly?" I ask again.

Instead of answering me, she walks by Dan and into the conference room.

*What. The. Actual. Fuck?*

My brain spins wildly. Chaotically. Nothing makes sense, yet it all makes perfect sense.

I don't know why she's here. *How is that possible?* Despite having so many unanswered questions and feeling scattered by that, I'm also ... relieved.

"Excuse me," I say to a man walking in my direction. From his vantage point, he had to have seen Kelly.

"Yes, Mr. Brewer."

"Can you tell me the names of the two women just standing here? Specifically, the one in the pink top?"

He nods, happy to assist. "Absolutely. The shorter one in the black shirt is Tally Thatcher. She's an intern in marketing. The other woman, the one in the pink top, is Aurora Johnson. She is ... was? ... Charlie McCabe's assistant."

*No. Fucking. Way.*

I pat him on the shoulder, my mind reeling. "Thank you for your help."

"Absolutely. Good to see you, sir."

I run my hand down my jaw and try to process this new piece of information.

Kelly's name is Aurora, and she works for my family.

Kelly's name is Aurora ...

*Oh my God. She did give me a fake name.*

My hand drops to my side, and a thousand thoughts run through my head like wildfire.

*What does this mean? Did she know who I was? Was she intentionally avoiding seeing me again?*

*Is this a strange coincidence?*

*Do my brothers know who she really is?*

I stare at the conference room door, licking my lips.

*Fuck.*

*The Situation*

It all makes sense to a certain degree. She was on the same flight from Nashville to Columbus, and the Raptors would've likely sent someone on their behalf to the same place. She did say she was going to a conference. I narrow my eyes, recalling our conversation from the plane. I think she mentioned working in marketing, too.

But I didn't see her on Saturday. *Wouldn't we have run into one another at some point?* It's like she disappeared sometime Saturday morning.

Or like she was avoiding me.

Dan pokes his head into the hallway and finds me. "We're ready whenever you are, Mr. Brewer."

*"The other woman, the one in the pink top, is Aurora Johnson. She is ... was? ... Charlie McCabe's assistant."*

I nod as a plan coalesces in my head.

"If you'll excuse me, I need to make a quick call," I say, smirking. "It'll just be a couple of minutes."

"Sure. We'll be here."

I nod and turn away, finding Gannon's number in my missed call log. He answers on the second ring.

"Hey," I say before he can even say hello. "What's the plan to replace McCabe again?"

"What?"

"McCabe. What's the plan?"

"We're looking for an interim replacement and hope he comes back."

My jaw tenses. "Stop looking for his replacement."

I hold my breath and wait for his response. Because if my brothers know that Kelly and Aurora are the same person and that she works for the hockey team, there will be a crack in Gannon's armor. He's a brilliant businessman, but he's a shit liar.

"Excuse me?" he asks, completely confused.

I exhale in relief. *They don't know.*

"Let me do it," I say.

"Let you do what?"

"Let me have his job."

He laughs. "Stop fucking around."

"*I mean it*. I can fill in for him. You said so yourself—you have no leads. You said a few days ago that you need a brother who understands hockey. I'm your guy."

"You don't know shit about hockey."

"Sure, I do."

*I don't. But things are about to get pucking fun around here.*

There's a pause. "Why? Why do you want to do this?"

"I feel bad for sending you to voicemail this morning."

"No, you don't."

"Just let me do this," I say. "My degree is in marketing, so it makes sense. And I'll still travel if you need me to but let me handle this for the time being."

He groans. "You know what? Fuck it. Fine."

*Score!* I balk. *Goal, maybe?*

"I don't even care anymore," Gannon says. "I just don't want to deal with it. If you want to handle the Raptors, be my guest."

I turn around and head toward the waiting Raptors employees.

"Thanks, Gan."

"The pleasure is all mine."

I end the call and then head to the conference room.

Let the fun begin.

# Chapter Thirteen

## Aurora

"Grab a seat," Dan says, pulling out a chair at one end of the table. "Mr. Brewer will be with us in just a second."

*Mr. Brewer? You've got to be fucking kidding me.*

Tally takes a seat beside me in the middle of the long table. Two of our coworkers, Jackson and Derek, take their seats across from us, absorbed in a conversation about hockey stats. Even if I wanted to pay attention to their back-and-forth right now, I couldn't.

There's no way. Every brain cell I have is being used.

I force a swallow, ignoring Tally's curious look. I can't explain to her right now that Mr. Brewer is none other than Tate Brewer—the Tate that thinks I'm Kelly Kapowski. That of all the days for him to make his first appearance in the Raptors offices and introduce himself, he chose today.

*How is this possible? How is this my life right now?* I tried one time to have a good time and do what other women do, and this is what I get.

I get fucked every which way, no pun intended.

"Hey, are you okay?" Tally whispers.

My smile feels about as real as this situation does. I shake my head slowly from side to side.

Her face drops. "What's wrong?"

She's rightfully confused because just a little while ago, I was as light as a feather. My smile was genuine, and my outlook on life positive. I was floating on a cloud built of memories of mind-blowing orgasms.

Too bad I didn't know that the giver of said orgasms would be sitting next to me, wondering why everyone is calling me Aurora. Knowing that would've dampened my spirits a bit.

"Aurora?" she whispers, prompting me to answer her question.

"Later," I say softly.

My eyes are glued to the double doors leading to the hallway. Heat stings my cheeks, and I place my hands on my lap so no one can see them shaking.

I have no idea what Tate is thinking. I only know the look in his eye just a moment ago wasn't precisely the bedroom eyes I saw this weekend. Moreover, I'm unsure how I feel about all of this. *Why can't I have a pause life button to give me a minute to get my thoughts together?*

The doors swing open with a flourish, and I jump in my seat. Tally gives me a curious look before trailing my gaze to the man walking into the room like he owns the place.

Because, apparently, he does.

*What the fuck?*

"I'm sorry to keep you waiting," Tate says, looking like a snack in dark pants and a green button-up shirt. It's the same emerald color of his eyes just before he comes.

*Now isn't the time to be thinking about that, Aurora.*

I shift in my seat, willing the knot in my stomach to ease.

*The Situation*

Air struggles to fill my lungs as Tate's gaze lands roughly on me. It's heavy. It's intentional. And it's chock-full of questions.

But as I squirm in my seat, feeling guilty as hell about lying to him about my name, and worried he'll think I tried to pull a fast one over on him by screwing the owner of the company, I realize something: I have questions, too.

I level my gaze with his, only to receive a barely lifted brow in return.

"That's not a problem," Dan says, rocking back in his chair as Tate sits to my right.

I take a deep breath, searching for the notes of his cologne that I've longed for all weekend. He leans forward to place his coffee and a notepad on the table. It's enough movement to fill my senses with amber and vanilla.

*Lord, help me.*

"Do you want to take the lead on this, or do you want me to explain why we're here?" Dan asks Tate.

"Why don't you do the honors?" Tate asks, his gaze sliding back to me.

"Excellent," Dan says. "Team, as most of you have probably heard by now, Charlie McCabe has taken a leave of absence. There was a family emergency on the West Coast. We hope to have him back once things are situated, but right now, it's up in the air."

"I'm sorry to hear that," Jackson says.

"Where does that leave us in the rebrand?" Derek asks.

"We're charging full steam ahead," Dan says.

Jackson glances at me. "The visual deck just came in from the art department for the logo, colors, and mascot."

"Charlie saw those come in before he left and made notes. They're on my desk. I'll send those to you as soon as we finish here," I say.

"Great," Jackson says.

"Do you happen to know when we can expect a final report from Good Day?" Derek asks. "We've been waiting on the market research for a week now, and Charlie said we should have it today."

Tally nods. "Yes. There's been a slight delay. I checked with Good Day's project manager this morning. The data has all come in, but it's still being analyzed. They amended the delivery date to Friday."

I look at Tate out of the corner of my eye. He's listening intently, as if this information fascinates him.

"I'm sorry," Tate says, the corner of his lip twitching. "I missed your name."

I bite my tongue. "Aurora Johnson."

"*Aurora Johnson.*" He says my name slowly, as if tasting it on his tongue. "You seem to have a solid grasp on what's happening here. What is it you do, exactly?"

"Mr. McCabe hired me to assist in the rebranding of the Raptors, specifically community engagement. While Derek and his team are working on more robust marketing strategies for the community at large, I'm focusing primarily on the fan experience."

"I'm a big believer in creating a memorable experience," Tate says, his eyes sparkling with mischief.

I steady myself, refusing to participate in whatever experience he's striving for now.

"How do we convert an average hockey fan into a Raptors super-fan?" I ask. "How can we turn the gameday experience into something special? How can we go into the community and build strong ties with our neighbors so they see us not as a money-grabbing sports franchise but a valuable tool that cares about the community?" I smile at him. "These are the questions I'm asking and hoping to answer."

"Don't let Aurora fool you," Dan says, beaming at me. "She's doing much more than that. She's also rebuilding our ... what do you call it? Spirit team?"

I nod. "We're leaning toward The Talon Team but haven't finalized that decision."

"Aurora is also McCabe's unofficial assistant," Dan says, looking at Tate. "This woman is a sponge. She soaks up everything you give her."

Tate fights a grin. "That's great to know."

I struggle not to roll my eyes.

"Who's the point of contact now?" Derek asks.

"We're working on that," Dan says. "McCabe's departure blindsided us, but we'll have an interim marketing director in place as soon as possible. Until then—"

"Actually, Dan," Tate says. "We've already found someone."

I don't know if it's how he says it, if the words are directed at me, or if I'm sensing the bomb that's dropping from the sky with a target on my lap, but for some reason, I brace myself.

"Really?" Dan asks, surprised.

Tate sits up. "I was just talking to Gannon, and we agreed that I'll be taking over McCabe's position for the time being."

*No, he didn't.* "You can't do that," I say before I can think it through.

All heads whip my way.

Tate smirks, lifting a brow. "And why not?"

"Aurora," Dan says, giving me a look that silently chastises me. "Mr. Brewer's family owns the Raptors. He can do whatever he wants."

I paste on a smile. "I'm sure he can. But I'm also certain that he has bigger problems than the marketing department we already have handled. I flew home Saturday afternoon and spent the entire evening with Charlie, as well as part of Sunday, taking notes."

"That's fantastic, *Aurora*," Tate says, making a point to say my first name. "You and I should sit down together so you can share all of that with me." He feathers his thumb over his kissable lips. "I have so many questions for you."

*I bet you do. But guess what, buddy? So do I.*

"Does anyone have anything to add?" Dan asks, pausing for us to jump in. When no one does, he shoves away from the table. "Very well. If that's it, then I guess all that's left to do is to welcome Tate to the team."

My stomach bottoms out.

Tally turns to me, her eyes as big as saucers.

*Yup, Tally. That's Tate.*

"*Aurora,*" she says, gasping. "Is that ...?"

"That would be him," I say softly as everyone stands and shakes Tate's hand.

"*Oh my God.*"

I round the opposite end of the table in hopes I can avoid Tate. Before I can get to the door, Tate's voice rises above the footsteps of my coworkers leaving the room.

"Aurora, if you could stay back, I would appreciate it," he says.

*Fuck.* "Of course."

My stomach flutters, and I can't decide if it's from dread or excitement.

I focus on keeping my breath steady as the room clears. As each body leaves, the space is filled with tension so thick it could be cut with a knife. The walls get closer. The temperature skyrockets.

Finally, we're alone.

As my gaze finds Tate's, all I can think about are the things we did this weekend.

The feel of his tongue between my legs. The taste of his cum on my tongue. The way his hands grabbed my hips as he held me in place and pounded into me at the perfect pace.

I want to do them again. *Now.*

"So *Aurora,* was it?" he asks, leaning against the table.

I cross my arms over my chest, struggling to erase the vivid imagery lingering in my mind. "Mr. *Brewer,* was it?"

"Don't come at me with that."

"Why not?" I ask. "It's not like you were being completely truthful with me, either."

"Omitting my last name is much different from lying about who I am."

## The Situation

"Is it, though? Because if you had told me that you were Tate *Brewer*, it might've set off a few alarms in my brain."

"Or you could've just told me you were Aurora Johnson and not some cheerleader from a cartoon."

"Would that have mattered? Would my name have meant anything to you? Do you sign every paycheck of every person who works under the Brewer umbrella of companies, and would've been able to pick out mine?"

He glares at me with a hint of amusement ghosting his lips.

"That's what I thought." I shrug. "This really is on you when you think about it."

The greens overtake the blues in his eyes. "There has been a lot on me in the past few days when it comes to you, most of it wet and sticky, and I don't feel guilty about any of it."

*Damn.*

I grab the edge of the table behind me so I don't dissolve into the floor.

"What are you thinking right now?" he asks, adjusting his tie.

I wonder if he's doing it to keep his hands busy so he doesn't reach for me. I hold the table tighter so I don't reach for him.

"What am I thinking?" I ask. "I'm thinking that this is the craziest coincidence on the face of the planet."

"I don't believe in coincidences."

"I do." I release the table and move around the room to dispel some of the energy zipping through my veins. "How else do you explain that the first time I choose to sleep with a random guy, he turns out to be my boss?"

He shrugs. "I think some people use the word *fate* or *kismet*, but feel free to substitute whatever makes you happy. I've discovered that you typically prefer *harder* and *deeper*."

I heave a breath. "Don't."

My heart pounds as I take in this delicious man whom I've not been able to stop thinking about for days.

It would be so easy to fall into his arms and let him ravage me again. The thought is almost too tempting to deny. My saving grace is our location—that our run-in happened at work, one job that I love and has given me so much meaning in this season of my life. It forces me to take a second. To breathe. To honestly consider what I'm doing.

With the moment of pause comes clarity through the haze of pheromones.

There was a reason I got up Saturday morning and left him asleep in his bed. And I can't forget that now—especially now when my job could be affected by my decision, too.

"Tate, I love this job. It's the best thing that's ever happened to me."

He cocks a brow as if he's challenging my declaration. But I don't react. I just move on.

"I had the best night with you," I say. "And I'm sorry if leaving you in the morning without saying goodbye was disrespectful. I didn't mean it that way."

"It did hurt my feelings."

I grin at the playful look on his face.

"Do you want to hash this out over dinner?" he asks. "That would really help me heal from the trauma of waking up alone."

"No."

"Why?"

I sigh. "I told you why. One-night stands don't come with an encore, no matter how amazing the performance."

"You thought it was amazing?" he asks, grinning from ear to ear.

*This man.* I shake my head.

"I had the best night of my life with Kelly." He winks. "And I'd do just about anything to see her again."

"Well, Kelly can't see you again, even if she agrees that it was the best night of her life, too."

"Why the hell not?" he asks.

I laugh softly. *Has he ever been told no?* "Because Kelly has a lot

## The Situation

of baggage. Kelly is trying to avoid repeating harmful patterns in her life. Kelly is trying to grow—and keep her job."

"Well, Tate with No Last Name would like to help her do all of those things."

"Tate with No Last Name just sees her as a challenge."

"That's not true."

He cuts the distance between us in half, close enough to be able to pull me to him.

Our proximity is infuriating. I'm pulled to him like a magnet, drawn to him like a rose to the sun. I crave the warmth his touch provides and feel myself leaning toward him to bask in his energy.

It would be so easy to give in. Yet I don't.

"You sell yourself short," he says, cupping the side of my face.

"How?"

"You think I'm interested in you because you're a challenge? If I wanted a challenge, I'd play golf."

I bite my lip to keep from giggling, but it's futile.

"Golf is one of the few things I'm not great at," he says, dropping his hand to his side. "I'd rather focus on putting my balls into other holes, if you know what I mean."

My laughter slips through the conference room. The sound makes him grin.

I wish that being with him, even in this setting, didn't feel so incredible. I'd give my right arm to be able to pull the fuse inside me that links his smile to my heartbeat so every time his lips tilt to the ceiling, my heart doesn't flutter.

I take a step back. "Can I ask you a question?"

"Sure."

"Did you take this job before or after you knew I worked here?"

"Does it matter?" he asks.

"Yes."

"Then after," he says with a simple shrug. "But, in my defense, my degree is in marketing, so it does make sense to take this on."

That's fair. And it is his company. "I want to keep working here, Tate."

"You better. I just took a job in hockey to be near you. I hate hockey."

I chuckle, both at his words and the look on his face. "But I need to know that what happened last weekend won't get me fired."

He steps back, observing me quietly, and I'm not sure how to take it. My body tenses as I consider that he might realize that it'll never work with me here. Case in point: we can't even have this conversation without sexual innuendos, and I'm 1000 percent sure that's against company policy. And he *can* fire me without cause. I'm still technically in my probation period.

"By all accounts, you are the one holding this department together," he says. "You were very impressive today."

I give him a real, broad smile. It grows wider when he doesn't lessen his praise by cheapening it with a nod to last weekend.

"If one of us needs to leave, it should be me," he says. "And I will leave if my presence here bothers you. I'll figure out a remedy because I refuse to make you feel uncomfortable, Aurora."

My mouth goes dry. "Thank you."

He glances at the floor for a moment, then lifts his gaze to mine. His eyes are clear, shining a bright blue, as he looks at me.

"I don't understand why you're trying to resist me," he says cheekily. "But let's put that aside for now."

"Nothing can happen between us again."

"I hear you."

"I mean it," I say, unflinching. "I'm the hero in my story. I have to save myself."

"You have to save yourself from what?"

I shrug. "Myself. I'm a romantic at heart and have a habit of falling for the first man who crosses my path when I'm vulnerable. And traditionally speaking, the first man to cross my path isn't the one for me."

"That makes total sense."

"Good."

"It seems as though a few motherfuckers cut in line."

My heart flutters despite my ferocious attempt at resisting him.

"But I do hear you," he says, searching my eyes as if he's trying to read me. "And I give you my word that not only is your job safe but you are also safe with me."

"I'm not with you, Tate."

He flashes me a sideways grin. "As your friend and boss, of course."

We both know that's not what he meant. We also know that I can argue with him until I'm blue in the face, and it won't change anything.

He's under my skin. *Deep.*

Goose bumps break out across my skin as a bout of anxiety hits me full-on. Tate was supposed to be my spicy little secret, a moment in time to bridge two eras of my life together. He wasn't supposed to be a fixture in my life.

And he wasn't supposed to make me feel anything but satisfied.

*What did you really think would happen when you picked* him *to share the night with, Aurora, you fool?*

Oof.

"Fine," I say, picking up my things from the table. "We're both adults. We're capable of a working relationship."

"Absolutely."

"And on that note, I need to get back to my office," I say, heading for the door. "I'll email you this afternoon with a revised schedule for this week."

I plant a hand on the door to push it open when Tate calls out. "Aurora."

My heart leaps in my chest as I stop pushing. "Yeah?"

"You could've left me half of the pie."

I snort, shaking my head, and walk out.

## Chapter Fourteen

Aurora

> Me: Tell me you're off tonight.

Jamie's answer is immediate.

## *The Situation*

Jamie: I should be done around six. Need to clean the salon, though. It's been a week already, and it's only Monday.

Me: I'll come by and help.

Jamie: Bring wine.

Me: Try whiskey.

Jamie: 😵

Me: It's been that kind of day.

Jamie: 🥃

# Chapter Fifteen

## Aurora

"Hey," I say, entering the salon from the back. The familiar smells and sounds from the old building help recenter me from the day's chaos. No matter where I work or how much I love working elsewhere, The Luxe will always be home. "Where are you, Jamie?"

I peek into her office. The light is on, but the room is empty.

"I'm in the front," she calls back.

"Today has been a day, and I mean *a day*," I say, traipsing through the building with a wine bottle swinging in my hand. "Wait until you hear this. It's going to blow your mind."

"If you could give me just a few minutes before you blow my mind, that would be great," she says. "Unless, of course, you don't mind Curtis hearing your story."

I round the corner and wince. A man sits in her chair with a cape covering his chest. He's probably a little older than us, but handsome in a slightly distinguished way.

"Sorry," I say, giving him a little wave. "I didn't realize Jamie still had a client."

"It's no problem at all." He nods toward the bottle at my side. "What kind of wine is that, if you don't mind my asking?"

"Cheap and red."

"She was supposed to bring whiskey," Jamie says, dusting his neck. "I'm not sure how to read the fact that she opted for wine instead."

I plop down in the chair my clients sit in when I'm working. "It's simple. I have to drive home and work tomorrow. As much as this day warrants whiskey, wine is the more responsible option."

"If you ever want pointers on vino, I'd be happy to share my knowledge with you," Curtis says. "I'm somewhat of a wine connoisseur."

Something about how he says it makes me want to laugh—not with him, but at him. *Who calls themselves a wine connoisseur? And unless you're Italian—which I'd bet he's not, who says vino?*

"We're more like amateurs instead of experts when it comes to wine," Jamie says. "As long as it does its job, we're happy."

"You ladies are missing out," Curtis says. "Wine is an experience."

I choke, pressing a hand to my chest as I hack up a lung. *Curtis, the best wine on earth doesn't hold a candle to the experiences I've had as of late.*

"Are you okay, Aurora?" Jamie asks, watching me curiously.

"Yeah." I clear my throat, patting my chest. "Excuse me."

Jamie removes Curtis's cape, and he gets to his feet. He's shorter than I would've guessed, and thinner than I imagined. I might've been vaguely interested in him if I didn't just leave the sexiest man alive.

I groan at the thought.

This is so unfair—to me and to every man I meet in the future. I can't compare them all to Tate. He can't be the bar by which other men are measured. No one stands a chance.

*Settle down, Aurora. This is your newfound libido talking. Tate might be gorgeous, sexy, sweet, and an absolute legend in bed, but Lewis and Kent both seemed wonderful at first, too. Give it time.*

I sigh. I'm either a sucker for punishment or a terrible judge of male character.

Come to think of it, I might be both.

"Here you go," Curtis says, handing Jamie a few crisp bills. "Great work."

"Thank you."

"I'll call you in about six weeks," he says.

"Sounds like a plan."

He nods. But instead of leaving, he turns to me.

I have the sudden urge to run. It's not out of fear—I could probably take ole Curtis with my shears if I had to. It's more of a disinterest in conversing with him. I came to talk to Jamie about Tate, not chitchat with a self-described wine connoisseur.

"Aurora, right?" he asks.

"That's right."

He smiles broadly. "Would you be interested in going out for dinner on Wednesday night?"

Jamie makes a face as she sweeps around her chair.

I start to turn him down. *Who goes on a dinner date in the middle of the workweek?* My lips part with a practiced speech about being too busy to date right now, but thanks for the offer. But before those words can come, I stop myself.

*Why turn him down? Is he my dream man? No.* But I'm supposed to be making sure that I sample the goods before I settle down again, and I've never dated a vino lover before. Maybe it's what I'm into.

I snort, covering it with a cough. *It's not what I'm into.* But at least I won't be home rotting and dreaming of Tate. That's the real objective.

I think.

## The Situation

"Why not?" I say, returning his smile as widely as I can. "Let's do it."

Jamie mutters something under her breath.

Curtis's face lights up. "Would you like to go anywhere specifically?"

"I like about everything."

"I really prefer that you pick the place, so I know you'll enjoy it."

"Okay," I say, wishing he had taken the lead and made the decision. "How about Leo's downtown?"

He frowns. "Sorry, but I'm not really into seafood."

"*Okay*. How about Caesar's?"

"That's fine."

*Don't sound too excited. You could've picked the place if you had this many feelings over the location.*

"What time?" he asks. "Let's do it before seven. It's so much cheaper in the evening." He taps the side of his head. "Gotta save where you can so you can have more money for vino."

*Oh my God. Help me. Please.*

I look at Jamie, regretting my decision already. She shakes her head, amused.

"Six," I offer, trying not to cringe. *If he can't make it at six, I'll back out.*

"I think I can make six," he says. *Great.* "Should we meet there?"

"Sure."

"Awesome. I'll see you then, Aurora. Goodbye, Jamie."

She nods. "Bye, Curtis."

I hold my breath and Jamie holds her broom, neither of us moving or speaking until the door closes behind him.

"What the hell was that?" I ask, slumping back into my chair.

"Did you not read my face? I was telling you to say no. And don't lie because I know my face speaks for me."

I hand her the bottle of *vino*. "I did read your face, but I chose to ignore it. That's apparently what I do now. I ignore every gut instinct and sign from the universe."

My brain sorts through a plethora of things I've done in the past few days that I shouldn't have because I knew better.

Converse with Tate on the plane. Staging a run-in with him at Ruma. Going to his room and letting him bend me into a pretzel. I snuck out, ignored my boss's calls, and ate half of a pie in my hotel room with a plastic spoon. Even though it was the best damn pie I've ever tasted, it still made me nauseous the whole flight home. And then I agreed to work under the guy I just laid under like I have some magical ability to separate the two.

The list goes on and on.

Jamie locks the door and flips the sign around to Closed. Then she heads into the back and retrieves two wineglasses that we hide for nights we hang out and clean, organize, or work late.

"So guess what happened to me today," I say, accepting a glass of wine from her.

"I wouldn't know where to start."

"Start with the wildest coincidence that you can imagine. Really let your mind wander. Be creative."

The phrase *creative juices* comes to mind, and I wonder if this is the rest of my life. *Will something happen every day to bring me back to the less than twenty-four hours I spent with Tate?*

She sips her drink, wheels spinning in her head. "You're pregnant."

"What? *No.* Why would you even say that?"

"It meets the parameters. It would be wild, and a coincidence since you've just started being active sexually again. It's also creative."

I down half of the glass of wine, willing the alcohol to hit and wear down the edge of my nerves. Jamie reaches over to give me a refill.

"No, I'm not pregnant," I say, shaking my head. "I hate you for even saying that."

"Why?"

"*Why?* Why would you even put that into the universe? If I'm going to be a mother, I'd like for it to be with someone I'm in a serious relationship with, not some guy I decided to bang one random night."

Because Tate would be the daddy.

An image of him carrying a sweet little nugget tries to enter my mind, but I punch it back like my worst enemy. Definitely *not* going there.

"That's fair." She grins devilishly. "But I can't help but love the fact that you just said those words. *Not some guy I decided to bang one random night.* My baby girl is back."

I roll my eyes. "Your baby girl isn't back. First, I'm not your baby girl. And second, I've never been this person, so I can't be back."

"Semantics."

"Can we get back to my day, please?" I ask, the wine beginning to warm my cheeks.

She takes a drink, telling me with her eyes to continue.

"So I went to work this morning, and we had a meeting," I say. "We were supposed to learn what was going to happen now that my boss left."

"Okay. Where are we going with this?"

"Well," I say, setting my glass down. I can't be trusted to hold it at this point in the story. "Guess who's filling in for Charlie?"

"No clue."

"*Tate.*"

She slow blinks.

"*Tate, Jamie.* The hottie from this weekend."

Her jaw drops to the floor. "*No.*"

"Yes."

"How?"

I cross one leg over the other and get settled in. "Apparently, Tate's last name is Brewer. As in, *he's part owner of the franchise.*"

Jamie gasps. "You banged a billionaire?"

I burst out laughing. "I guess so. I hadn't thought of it like that."

"You're the new Anastasia Steele."

My stomach clenches at the visual that pops up in my head. Being tied up has never appealed to me before, but now ...

I shiver.

"How is this working out?" Jamie asks. "Was he cool with it?"

*"I had the best night of my life with Kelly."* He winks. *"And I'd do just about anything to see her again."*

I laugh, blowing out a heavy breath. "Oh, he's cool with it."

She narrows her eyes suspiciously.

"This man is something else," I say. "He wasn't supposed to take this position. He only did it after he realized I worked there."

"Why do the gods love you so much?"

I laugh again.

"How did he take finding out you're not Kelly Kapowski?" she asks.

"I think he was shocked. Probably a little irritated. But I was shocked and irritated, too, that he withheld his last name from me—which, may I point out to you like I did to him, was a much bigger deal."

"And let me go out on a limb here and say that you have decided to take this once-in-a-lifetime situation and have an adverse reaction to it."

I give her a look, warning her to tread lightly, and take another large gulp of wine.

"I'm starting to think you enjoy sabotaging yourself," she says.

"It's not that. You haven't seen him, Jamie. He's too perfect. He's too ... gah!" I get to my feet, unable to sit still any longer. "He's trouble—a walking heartbreak that I don't need in my life."

"Maybe you do need it."

My eyes bulge. "What's that supposed to mean?"

She shrugs noncommittally. "When have you ever lived dangerously?"

"I just took a date with Curtis, for fuck's sake. That's living dangerously if I ever heard it."

"No, that was just ... again, self-sabotage."

*The Situation*

I roll my eyes. "I had a one-night stand. That was dangerous, and that's what got me here."

"Welcome to the real world where, statistically speaking—because I did look this up—nearly half of all women our age have had one."

She pauses, giving me time to refute her claim. But I don't.

"Listen, Ror. As your best friend, I'm saying this with love. But take a step back and look at this from an outside perspective. You've told me since the day you left Kent that you want to do something different with your life. Now, you've done it, and you're scared. New things are supposed to be scary."

I exhale, wishing I could argue that, too.

"You have had more spark, more energy—more passion—in the past few days than I might've ever seen you possess in all the years I've known you. You've given me every indication that you like this billionaire bad boy," she says. "Am I reading this wrong?"

Everything in me wants to say no. I want to deny that she's right and pretend I don't want Tate. But that would be a big fat lie.

*I do want him.* I'm not surprised by that, because I knew I would. From the moment he turned to me and smiled, I knew I was playing with fire. But I can't see anything ending well between the two of us, and if I've learned anything, it's that I have to protect myself.

No one else is going to do it, that's for damn sure.

"Yes, I like him," I admit because it's pointless to lie to my best friend. "But that doesn't mean it's smart or healthy."

"You have to start trusting yourself."

"I do. That's why I'm putting up barriers and holding them tight."

"Right. Because people put up barriers because they trust themselves so damn much. Got it."

I glare at her.

"Look, I'm on your side no matter how goofy you get," she says. "And I do agree that you have to be smart when it comes to men." She leans forward. "But I also think you have to be smart when it comes to you. This guy, Tate, has been great to you, and you're denying yourself fun ... why?"

No matter what I say, it's going to sound dumb. So I don't bother.

After a long soak in the bath and a couple of cocktails on Sunday night, I called Jamie and filled in the gaps from our *walk of shame* conversation on Saturday morning. I was relaxed and a little freer with my thoughts and feelings than I probably should've been. I think it painted a picture that might be a little too ... accurate.

"I'm not denying myself anything," I say. "I'm just giving myself new opportunities for adventure."

She snorts. "You mean Curtis?"

"Yeah. I mean Curtis."

She downs the rest of her drink and grabs the broom again.

"Do you think Curtis is going to be the guy to bring you passion and love and affection?" she asks. "Or is the vino connoisseur your next lover boy?"

The thought makes me want to gag.

"No," I admit. "I don't necessarily think he fits any of those qualifiers. But he is closer to my age and less likely to break my heart."

"Weren't you supposed to be picky this time around?"

"Yes, and I am. I intentionally chose a man who would provide me with something else to think about."

"Besides the guy you really like, right?"

She hums.

I hum back at her.

This is a mess—a big ole mess. But I'm determined not to let my attraction to my boss derail my new direction in life.

*I can handle this. I've got this.*

I also fear that I *am* lying to myself.

# Chapter Sixteen

## Aurora

"I don't like any of them." I scroll back to the first page of uniform designs. "They're just lackluster. There's nothing iconic or fun about any of these." I glance over my shoulder at Tally, who is standing behind me. "What do you think?"

"I can't disagree with you. I don't know how they missed the mark so badly. These are unfortunate."

"Take this one, for example," I say, pointing at the design in the center of the screen. "Nothing about this pops. It's completely generic."

"It's better than this one." Tally motions toward the last one displayed on my computer screen. "I'm not sure where they were even going with this. If I were a child at a hockey game and someone ran up to me wearing this, it would've scared the bejesus out of me."

"The one beside it is three strips of fabric. I don't know what they'd charge for this, but if it's over ten dollars, it's too much."

Tally sighs, moving around my desk and sitting across from me. She pulls her computer onto her lap and starts typing away.

"I'm just making some notes before I forget," she says. "I'll respond to their email with our comments and ask them to try again. I'll ensure you're cc'd."

"Thank you. Maybe try emphasizing that we want something fresh and fun."

"And family friendly." She looks at me over the screen and grins. "Should I insist that they use a minimum of five strips of fabric?"

I laugh, switching from my email to my online calendar. "Now let's review the audition schedule. You reserved the facilities for the dates in blue, correct?"

"Right. I have a tentative hold on the dates in yellow, too, just in case. It's so hard to snag times. I figured it was better to have more and not need them than not have them and be screwed."

"Absolutely. We're announcing everything next week. Are we ready to go on that?"

Tally finishes her typing with a flourish. "Yup. Ready to go. We have new Social accounts and an amazing new website to launch on Monday. I'll have a few posts for you to approve in a day or two. Derek was going to use Good Day's research to help tailor the posts to our targeted demographic, but the report, as you know, is delayed."

"Okay. Applications open on Saturday, correct? And we're doing that through a portal on the website?"

"Exactly. The tech team is adjusting the back end of the website, which I don't fully understand, but they expect it to be completed by Wednesday." She looks up. "Guess it should be done tomorrow."

Bile creeps up my throat as I think about Wednesday.

"You just turned a little green," Tally says, confused.

"I'm fine. I just ..." I sigh. "I have a date on Wednesday night at six with a guy I should never in a million years have agreed to see."

"Then why did you?"

"Because I hate myself, apparently." I look at the ceiling. "We're going to Caesar's at six."

"That's … an interesting choice."

"Yeah. Let's move this conversation along, please. I'm going to pretend this date isn't happening until the very last minute."

She side-eyes me like I might fall apart but does as requested. "Additionally, I reviewed your notes from last week on the audition process, and I'm not sure I fully understood them. Do you have a moment to go over it?"

"Of course."

My email dings and a new message from Tally is at the top.

"Take a look at that," she says. "I tried to organize it in the most logical way possible. Feel free to adjust it, obviously."

I scan her notes. "Okay, let's start day one with something fun. Maybe Raptors trivia, just to break the ice. Let's do games while the interviews are happening, and let's do those in groups of three. That'll give us insight into how they act in a group setting. The games will single out who will partake in activities and who won't."

"Oh, that's smart."

"I've done this before." I smile. "Granted, I was on the other side of things, but the process is the process."

"Do you want the choreography for day two to go to everyone on the first day? Or wait and see who gets cut and send it only to those who make it?"

"If they don't make it to the second day, they don't need the choreography. Let's make sure someone tapes the routine, and we'll send it via text or email to everyone we ask back for day two."

"Got it."

I look up at a knock on the door.

"Excuse me, ladies. Am I interrupting?" Tate grins from the doorway.

*Does this man ever not look good?*

Dark gray pants paired with a crisp white T-shirt make for a striking combination. The man does rock a good white shirt. A black blazer matches a black belt wrapped around his waist. Bright white sneakers tie the look together.

He looks like he walked straight off a runway.

He steps inside my office, and I'm immediately hit with a burst of his cologne. I don't know whether he wore an extra spritz today, or if I'm just acutely aware of everything about him. Either way, the scent has my mouth watering.

"We were just making changes to the audition process for the promo team," Tally says, looking up at him with stars in her eyes.

I don't blame her. Everyone in the office reacts to him, albeit in different ways. Some women drool. Some men chase him like puppies. Others stand back in awe like they're watching a movie. Porn, probably.

He does this simply by existing. *What kind of magic is that?*

Tate slides a hand in his pocket and casually leans against the door. "The promo team ... is that the talent team you were discussing yesterday?"

"It's tough to come up with a cute name when your mascot is a raptor," I say, laughing. "We're still throwing ideas around."

"I'm 99 percent sure that my father chose the mascot," Tate says. "That's par for the course considering everything that man touched turned to shit."

The office grows quiet, and I don't know what to say. It's never good to pile on when someone remarks negatively about their family. But the flash in his eyes when he mentioned his dad makes me curious.

"Aurora, if you don't mind, I'm going to head back to my desk and get started on these replies," Tally says.

"Great idea. If you need anything, let me know."

"I will." She grabs her computer and stands. "It was good seeing you, Mr. Brewer."

He gives her a dazzling, panty-dropping smile. "You, too, Tally."

She trips on a chair leg on her way out.

Tate shuts the door behind her.

"You wield that thing like a weapon," I say, sitting back in my chair.

"What *thing*?"

"That smile."

He sits on the corner of my desk. "I've smiled at you several times, and you seem to be defending yourself just fine."

If he only knew just how often I've gone to war with myself over his smile, among other things, he'd be surprised.

I look at him, smirking from his perch above me.

*No, he wouldn't.*

I wondered how often we'd see each other during the normal course of the day. He was nowhere to be found when I arrived at six thirty this morning. I saw him briefly after lunch, but a little wave was our only form of connection. A part of me feels relieved that I haven't seen him a lot ... and another part of me is disappointed.

"How has your day been?" he asks.

I glance around the mess on my desk. "Productive. One of my superpowers is being productive when I'm avoiding something."

"Don't you mean some*one*?"

I grin. "Are you insinuating that I'm avoiding you?"

"Have you been avoiding me?"

"Not specifically," I say.

"And to think that my goal has been trying to run into you all day," he says, his eyes sparkling. "This doesn't bother you, does it? Me being in your office? Because if it does, I'll go."

I wish I could say that it did, but it would be a lie. Because every time someone has passed my doorway today, I've held my breath, hoping it was him. And that is the problem. We get along so well. If things were different, I can easily imagine being friends with Tate Brewer. He's fun, his sense of humor is on point, and his wit is perfection. He's also smart, kind, and respectful.

Damn him.

"No, it doesn't bother me," I say softly.

He pushes off my desk. "So what are you making for dinner tonight?"

"That's not at all random."

"You said you like to cook, so I was wondering what you make on a random Tuesday night."

"I have no clue. I haven't been able to give it much thought. Probably whatever is in my fridge."

He smiles. "I know this little place not too far from here where—"

"Tate."

"What?"

"No."

He sighs, frowning. "You've single-handedly turned me down more than every other woman in my twenty-seven years combined."

"You're twenty-seven?" *Oh God.*

"Yeah." His brows tug together. "What's the big deal? How old did you think I was?"

"Honestly, I've intentionally not thought about it."

"As in, you made a point to not think about it because you care or because you don't care?"

I cover my face with my hands and release a long sigh.

"You realize I'm an adult, right?" he asks, grinning.

I drop my hands. "Yes, I realize that. That wasn't my concern. My concern was the age gap between us and just how excessive it might be because I don't really love feeling that much older than you."

"You're older than me?"

I flash him a look that earns me a mischievous grin. "You know damn good and well that I'm older than you."

"You're under the wrong assumption that I've given your age a lot of thought. I'd rather be thinking about doing very, *very* dirty things to that delectable body of yours and not two numbers denoting how many years you've walked on Earth. That's far less interesting."

My body reacts to him without my permission. Heat pools in my cheeks and my core, and my breaths begin to tremble. My heart pounds as all internal systems prepare for an encounter it's not going to get.

"Look at you," he says just loud enough for me to hear. "This is how I have to get the truth out of you."

"What are you talking about?"

"You may lie to me, but your body? It doesn't, and it really likes me, Aurora."

Hearing my name—my real name—slip past his lips in a sentence so heady rips down the shield I've been trying to hold steady.

I keep dancing around the truth, and all that's getting me is peppered with questions. I'm not sure if he's seeing how much it'll take to get me to crack, or maybe he likes watching me squirm. Either way, if I level with him, perhaps we can find a way to work through this predicament we've found ourselves in.

"Okay, Mr. Brewer." I look him in the eyes. "Let's just put it all out on the table and get it over with."

"Like we did the other night, or …"

*God.* I lick my bottom lip. "I find you insanely attractive."

His eyes shift to my favorite emerald-green hue.

"I replay last weekend over and over in my head. And if things were different—if I were different, if we were different ages—I'd entertain you and your theatrics. But things are not different, Tate. There are numerous reasons this can't work, and to add to that, I now work for you. It's probably illegal for us to even be having this conversation right now."

He snorts. "You clearly haven't met my family. Three of my brothers married women they worked with, and my sister married her bodyguard. I'm not sure if that means we work too much or what, but it does seem to work out for us." He laughs. "My point in telling you this is that I assure you there's no handbook violation. My brother Jason is too much of a rule follower. He would've had that section removed before he touched his assistant."

I laugh at the tenderness with which he discusses his family.

I've wondered many times what it would be like to have a large family. I often felt alone growing up. My parents were always at the church, working on sermons or leading a class. They hauled me with them. So instead of growing up with siblings or even a large group of similarly aged kids, I grew up with older people who thought children should be seen and not heard.

For the briefest moment, I again imagine Tate as a father, and my heart doubles in size.

"Why won't you give me a chance, Aurora?"

His features are smooth and sober. Long gone is the playfulness and mischief I'm used to seeing on his face. He's serious, and that takes my breath away.

The least I can do is be honest with him.

"I'm too scared," I say, shrugging like I just told him the sky was blue. I may look nonchalant, but my insides break open as I speak my truth aloud.

He stills. "You're scared of me?"

"I'm scared of you. I'm scared of me. I'm scared of even considering falling for someone again. Not that that's what you're asking me to do, of course. I'm not implying that you've somehow fallen for me in such a short period because that would be ridiculous."

"Maybe it would be," he says, searching my eyes. "But wouldn't it also be ridiculous to allow fear to hold you back from something that has the potential to be amazing?"

His words hit my heart, striking the middle of my wounds.

He's right. Allowing fear to hold me back is ridiculous. *But isn't it equally unreasonable to jump into deep, dark waters without thinking it through?*

"Why do you care so much, Tate? Isn't this more trouble than it's worth?"

I force a swallow. *Aren't I more trouble than I'm worth?* I hate that thought, but it's right there, festering inside me.

"You mean, aren't *you* more trouble than *you're* worth?"

I fill my lungs with air and hold it, feeling the burn of the expansion overtake the sting of embarrassment at being called out.

*The Situation*

His phone rings, breaking the silence between us. His gaze lingers on me for a long moment before he pulls the device from his pocket.

"I need to take this," he says, looking at the screen.

I can't find my voice, so I just nod.

He slips out of the room, closing the door behind him.

# Chapter Seventeen

# Tate

"I think she thought our conversation was over," I say, pinching the edge of the pie crust for Mimi.

She sits next to me at her kitchen table, studying my every move.

Mimi used to make a pie a week when I first met her. There would be a freshly baked pie or cobbler every Wednesday when I showed up for our date. But as time passed, the motor skills required to mix the ingredients, roll the dough, pinch the edges, and prep the filling—not to mention creating the fancy lattice crusts she's a big fan of—got to be too much. Instead of letting her feel bad about it, because she knew I loved her pies, I teased her and told her that I knew what she was doing. She wanted to bake with me instead of for me.

That's not true, but I think she appreciated me saying it. And I've been the baker in our relationship ever since.

*The Situation*

"She'll come around," Mimi says. "I mean, look at you. You're hot stuff."

"I'd have to be hot stuff to pull a stunner like you."

She smacks my arm and laughs. "She's probably just playing hard to get, but she won't last long. God knows I wouldn't." She whistles between her teeth. "They didn't make men like you when I was young, I'll tell ya that."

"What do you think about age gaps, Mimi?" I ask, filling the pie shell with blueberry filling.

"What do you mean?"

"Aurora is older than I am. I don't know by how much, but I don't care. It's just a number."

"That's right."

I paint the crust with an egg wash. "She made a comment about being older than me and that it made her feel a certain way, I guess. I've been thinking about that a lot because it's one thing I can't fix."

"Oh, honey. That's something almost every woman thinks about at least once in their life."

"Fucking a younger man?" I ask, plopping the pie in the preheated oven and setting a timer.

She laughs. "Well, yes, that, too."

I turn on the tap and rinse the dishes before putting them into the dishwasher, all the while my thoughts are still with Aurora. I didn't see her in the office today. Jackson said she and Tally had meetings elsewhere and would be gone most of the day. Luckily, there was more than enough work to keep me busy—but not enough to keep her off my mind.

"I'd imagine that she's in a place in her life where she's been through some shit, survived even more shit, and she's now looking for a soft spot to land. But she doesn't trust anyone because everyone has let her down. And when she looks in the mirror, she's no longer young and beautiful in her eyes." Mimi's delicate shoulders lift and fall. "Being a woman can be hell."

"Try understanding one."

But as the words leave my mouth, I'm reminded of Aurora's mention of fuzzy blankets.

*"Instead of living my life in survival mode and just getting through each day, I'm trying to craft a life that feels good. Soft. Feminine. Like my life is wrapped in a fuzzy blanket, if that makes sense."*

She laughs. "Women aren't that complicated if you really want to understand them. This one sounds like she's not been valued or feels she's given more in her relationships than she's received. And she's going to make you work for it, Tate. You won't win this one over by pussyfooting around."

"I just want to be loved, dammit," I say, fake crying.

This makes Mimi shake her head and chuckle.

"I'm gonna tell you one thing right now," Mimi says, closing the dishwasher and starting it. "I can't have you hanging around here every week, moping about some girl. I'll share you with her, but I'm not sacrificing my Tate time to save hers. You're gonna have to shit or get off the pot."

My jaw drops. "I haven't even known her a week yet. Give me some time."

"Do ya listen to anything I say?"

"Every last word of it."

"Then start drawing the connections with that big brain of yours." She heaves a breath as she sits in her recliner on the other side of the bar. "She turned down dinner and then showed up. She told you it was only for one night, right?"

I nod, unsure where she's going with this.

"She left you the next morning," Mimi recalls. "She's telling you over and over that she doesn't believe that you'll continue to be there for her. I'd bet a dime to a donut that she's felt neglected in her previous relationships."

*"Why do you care so much, Tate? Isn't this more trouble than it's worth?"*

"Who knew you were a love guru?" I ask.

"You'd be surprised. I was quite the rascal back in the day."

## The Situation

"Mimi, I have no doubt."

I take my usual spot on the couch beside her recliner and watch a Western we've already seen several times. The weather is beautiful, so I figured she'd want to go on a golf cart ride and terrorize the neighborhood, but she hasn't mentioned it.

I study her, taking in the bags under her eyes and the spots on her skin. She's starting to look her age. She's beginning to look tired.

It scares the shit out of me.

When Jason married Chloe, her grandmother came with the package. Jason moved her into his renovated guest cottage so she could have her own space. Between me, Ripley, and Renn, I think she gets more visitors than our own mother.

If Mom would stay stateside longer than a week every two or three months, we could see her more often, too.

"We got a new security guy," Mimi says.

"Yeah, I heard that was happening. We received a memo a couple of months ago telling us that Landry Security was hiring new personnel and that we should expect to see new members on our security teams."

She points a bony finger at me. "Well, I don't like my new guy, and I told Jason as much."

"Who did you get?"

"This bastard named Callum."

I snort. *Oh, the infamous Callum.* "Say less, Mimi."

"Say less? What's that supposed to mean?"

I grab the remote off the coffee table and turn the movie down. "That means that you don't have to say anything else. I get it."

"Do you know him?"

"Unfortunately."

"Well, pull some strings for your woman over here and tell them I don't want Callum. I liked Grey. Can I just have Grey?"

"You just think Grey is cute."

"So? Let me look," she says, throwing up her hands. "I'm going to die soon. Let me get my kicks in while I can."

I shake my head and toss the remote back on the table.

"What's your plan?" she asks, her eyes glued to the television. The actor is her favorite—a baby-faced cowboy who, in real life, supposedly was badass. Mimi made me read his biography one time.

"What's my plan for what?"

She looks at me, annoyed. "I'd like to see you married and have kids before I kick the bucket. But your lackadaisical attitude is making me think that's not going to happen."

"Babe, I'm not being lackadaisical."

She flashes me an ornery grin at my use of her favorite pet name. "Do you want some tips?"

"Give them to me."

She twists in her chair to face me, her cowboys getting into a firefight in the distance. She tugs a blanket onto her lap.

"The first tip you'll be good at," she says. "You already do this for me."

I lean back, wide-eyed. "Have you been having dreams about me again?"

"No, you little shit." She laughs, tilting her head back. "I'm talking about bringing me food."

"That's a relief."

She shakes a finger playfully at me. "Men get it all wrong. Now, I can't speak for all women, but I will say that a lot of women can be won over through their stomach."

"Not the body part I was expecting, but I'm listening."

Mimi groans as she moves, favoring her right hip.

I watch her try to get comfortable and wish there was something that I could do to help her. I've often wondered if she gets lonely in this little cottage. She'd never admit it if she did—she's too proud for that. But I am curious from time to time if she wishes she had a husband or a boyfriend other than me.

"Food can be more intimate than sex," she says, picking at the neckline of her light blue dressing gown. "Because it's not about the food at all. It's about the thought and the care—not to mention the time that goes into it. When you bring me food every Wednesday, it makes me feel so important to you."

"Because you are. I love you."

She beams. "You know I love you, too, charmer." She rests her head against the chair and sighs happily. "This is why couples fight about where to eat. That's not the fight at all. It's the woman wanting the man to show her that he cares for her by providing this essential need—even if it's fast food. Just make the decision."

"Okay. That makes sense. I've never thought of it that way."

"Then adjust your thoughts because this is already in your wheelhouse. Just make sure you put it into play."

Whiffs of blueberries and pie crust slowly fill the home. It's the kind of smell I've always thought a mom's kitchen should have. Our kitchen growing up was scented like cleaning products from the housekeeper, and mine now is reminiscent of whatever I burned the night before while trying to make dinner.

But this? This is goals.

*I might just have to move Mimi in with me ...*

"The second tip is to work for it," she says. "Put in the effort. Be consistent. Show her that you're passionate and that you mean it. Go big or go home, as they say. Especially with this woman of yours. I think she needs that."

"Done."

"Third?" She grins with a hint of mischief. "Women love to see men with babies. It sets off something inside them that makes them start thinking about *having* babies, which leads to the bedroom for some hanky-panky."

"Hey," I say, grabbing my phone. "That's super smart and, lucky for me, I know a lot of people who have babies."

"Toss me that remote before you start thumbing that phone."

I hand it to her and then go back to my messages.

> **Me:** Hey, fam.
>
> **Jason:** Hi.
>
> **Renn:** Yo.
>
> **Bianca:** Hey, Tate!
>
> **Me:** I have a very serious favor to ask you.

Silence fills the chat. I'm about to try to re-engage them when Ripley responds.

> **Ripley:** To ask who?
>
> **Me:** All of you with a kid.
>
> **Renn:** 😳
>
> **Bianca:** *gulps*
>
> **Me:** I need to borrow one of them.
>
> **Jason:** One of what?
>
> **Me:** One of your kids.

I roll my eyes at their ineptitude. *Can't any of them follow along?*

"Do you see that guy?" Mimi asks, pointing at the screen.

I glance up to see five cowboys who all look the same. "Sure. What about him?"

"Can you imagine that guy fighting with his woman about where to eat? Hell, no. He's taking her to dinner and then back home to eat, if you know what I mean." She smirks. "And that's what women want."

*There's nothing I can say to that without painting a picture that does not need painted.*

*The Situation*

> Renn: Yeah, hard no. But thanks.
>
> Bianca: I'm in Florida. Sorry!
>
> Gannon: Did Tate just ask to BORROW A BABY?
>
> Ripley: 🫣

"Having any luck?" Mimi asks, her eyes pinned to her cowboy.
"Not yet. I'm working on it."
"That timer should be going off any second."

> Me: I don't need it for long. An hour, tops.
>
> Gannon: Did you just call my daughter an "it"?
>
> Jason: I'm so curious but too scared to ask questions.
>
> Ripley: You can borrow Pancake and Waffles.

"Do puppies work?" I ask Mimi.
"Yes, but they aren't as effective."

> Me: I'm happy to take them to the doggy park any time, but they won't work for this project.

> Gannon: Our children are not ... You know what? I'm not having this conversation.

> Me: You're hateful.

> Renn: Why do you need to borrow a baby?

> Ripley: Can we go to prison if we hear this explanation?

> Bianca: I don't think so ...

> Me: Mimi says that women love men who have babies. Well, not men who have babies but men who hold babies.

> Renn: Yeah, Arlo isn't available to be your wingman. Good idea, though.

> Me: It's not like you need him. You already have Blakely. You're being selfish.

The timer rings from the kitchen, and the blueberry smell grows thicker. My stomach rumbles as I get to my feet.

"My family won't share their kids," I say, offering my arm to Mimi. "They're so rude."

She loops her arm through my elbow. "I can't give you a baby, or I would." She shakes her head as we walk into the kitchen. "I'd give you ten babies, you little stud."

*Wow.*

"Where are my oven mitts?" she asks herself as she piddles around the room.

I sit at the table and catch up on the texts.

*The Situation*

> Ripley: I'd let you borrow my kid, buddy. But I don't have one.
>
> Gannon: You would not.
>
> Jason: On a serious note, we have a request for a jet for the Raptors next week. Do you still need that, Tate?

*How would I know?* A slow smile spreads across my lips. *But I do know someone who does ...*

My fingers fly across the keys.

> Me: No clue. Let me check on it.
>
> Jason: Do it ASAP, please. I have to send one to pick up Mom in France on the same day. It's a fine balance over here until all the aircraft are up and running.
>
> Me: I'll get back to you. The rest of you—go be stingy with your babies.

I click out of the chat before I can read their responses ... and because I have a great excuse to call Aurora.

My body buzzes as I imagine hearing her voice. I wonder if she has anything to say about our conversation yesterday. *Does she replay our chats like I do? Does she pick them apart to see what she might've missed?*

"Tate, this is one pretty pie," Mimi says, admiring my handiwork.

"It smells amazing."

"It's going to taste amazing, too. But we aren't cutting it until it cools, you little monkey."

"I cut one pie hot, and it's all you remember." I make a face at her. "I need to make a very important call."

She shoos me away with her hand as she heads to the recliner again. "Go outside because I'm about to turn this movie up."

I step outside onto her small concrete patio. The air is warm and still, and the sky is bursting with purples and pinks around the setting sun. But I don't have time to appreciate it.

I scroll through my contacts list to see whose number I have from the Raptors. I haven't bothered to save many contacts yet. The only one I can find is Tally's because I had to call her yesterday about some of Charlie's paperwork that went missing. Luckily, she knew where to find it.

The line rings once, twice, and then, on the third time, she picks up.

"Tally Thatcher," she says.

"Hey, Tally. It's Tate."

She clears her throat. "*Oh.* Good evening, Mr. Brewer."

"I'm trying to reach Aurora. Is she in the office?"

"Sir, it's five thirty. Everyone's gone but me and the cleaning crew."

I pace in a wide circle. "Why are you still there?"

"Because there's work that must be done."

*I really like this girl.*

"I told Aurora that I would take care of a few things so she could enjoy her night," she says.

She ends the sentence with a little dry laugh, almost as if she's sharing information she shouldn't be. *What's that about?*

"Do you have a number where I can reach her?" I ask, slowing my paces.

"Of course. But I wouldn't plan on reaching her tonight."

I stop moving. "And why is that?"

"Because she's on a date."

*She's on a what?*

My jaw pulses as my brain accepts this information.

*She's on a date? Aurora? What the fuck?*

"She left here about twenty minutes ago," Tally says. "There was

## The Situation

just enough time for her to run home, get cleaned up, and then get to Caesar's by six."

The way she says each word makes it clear she's intentionally dropping information.

*I really, really like this girl.*

"You know what? Forget the number," I say, my brain two steps ahead of her. "I'll contact Aurora another way."

"I think that sounds like a great idea, Mr. Brewer. You should do that."

I smile. "Tally?"

"Yes?"

"Go home. You've gone above and beyond today."

She laughs as I end the call.

## Chapter Eighteen

# Aurora

The light turns green, and I press on the accelerator so slowly that the car behind me honks.

I flip my visor down and squint into the low-hanging sun. The warmth feels good on my face and casts a positive glow around me. Too bad it doesn't work to rid me of the negative thoughts rolling through my mind.

Mostly ... guilt.

I press my lips together as I make a right-hand turn.

I don't owe Tate anything, and I've also been clear about not wanting anything. But that's the problem. I'm not certain that's wholly true anymore.

*"You mean, aren't you more trouble than you're worth?"*

My palm smacks against the steering wheel.

*How can he see right through me? And how much longer can I pretend he doesn't have a key that unlocks the box where I hold my deepest fears—a key he seems to want to use?*

He's wrinkled my plans and made me question everything I thought was true. It's uncomfortable. It's concerning. But it's also impossible not to acknowledge the effort he's putting forward.

"Why won't you give me a chance, Aurora?"

I pilot the car into Caesar's parking lot and find a spot near the door.

A lump settles in my throat. "I don't know Tate. I don't fucking know anymore."

*Isn't he objectively everything I've dreamed of in a man?* He's emotionally intelligent and kind. Patient. Respectful. He sees me and makes me feel like I matter. And, my God, can he make me come.

"What's really happening here?" I ask, turning off the car. "Why the hell am I going on this pseudo-date when everything I want is a phone call away?"

The answer trickles into my mind like a dark cloud.

*Because I don't know how to handle him.*

The realization makes my stomach woozy. My palms sweat. That single sentence cuts through the fog in my brain like a knife.

I don't know what to do with Tate. It's really that simple. *What happens when the answer to your prayers, the embodiment of your dreams, actually materializes? How does that work?*

*Worse, what if it doesn't work? What if everything you thought you wanted turns out to be wrong, and then you're left with nothing, not even a dream?*

I grab my purse off the passenger's seat, but I can't stop the thoughts from coming at me like a freight train.

I know what to do with men who talk a good game but don't walk it. I can handle men who say what I want to hear when I'm facing them but talk out of the other side of their mouth when I turn away. And I know what happens when a man love bombs you but is missing once the dust settles.

My breaths are shaky. "He's flipped the script. It's no longer that

I'm afraid of making the wrong decision. I'm actually afraid of making the right one."

A smile ghosts my lips as I get out of the car and head into the restaurant. I deliberately place one foot in front of the other, so I don't hop back into the car and flee the scene of what I'm fairly certain is going to be a crime.

The restaurant isn't busy, which is no surprise at this hour in the middle of the week. I've never felt so old in my damn life.

"Table for one?" A pretty blonde with a name tag reading Morgan approaches the hostess stand from the dining area.

I scan the room for Curtis. "No, actually, I'm supposed to be meeting someone here. Do you happen to know if there's a man waiting on a woman?"

"There's not. We only have three tables right now—two couples and a regular patron who always dines alone." She grabs two menus from a stack. "I could go ahead and seat you, if you'd like. Or you're welcome to wait out here. It's totally up to you."

I'm not sure what to do, but sitting alone feels slightly less awkward than standing near the door.

"A table would be great," I say.

Morgan lets me choose where to sit, and I select a booth in the corner. Something about having my back to a wall is comforting. She takes my drink order and leaves me with the menus.

I blow out a breath, surveying my surroundings. The place is nice and clean. The handful of other patrons seem to be comfortable and happy with their food. It's the kind of place that Kent would've taken me during our marriage. I'm not quite sure how to process that.

"Well, hello," Curtis says, materializing out of thin air. He slides in the booth across from me. "You must've been right on time."

"I was about five minutes early."

"I'm always fashionably late. It keeps people on their toes," he says, chuckling at himself.

Morgan appears with my glass of water. Her brow is furrowed, and I can only imagine what she's thinking.

*The Situation*

Curtis is slathered in a bottle of men's cologne. His freshly cut hair is slicked back in a style that's very unbecoming of him. He's not a bad-looking man, but he's not doing himself any favors with the attempted mustache.

"Hello to you," he says to Morgan.

She stands next to me. "Can I get you something to drink?"

"Do you have a vino menu?" he asks.

*Oh good God.* I rub my forehead.

"Excuse me?" she asks, rightly confused.

"Wine," I say, dropping my hand to my side. "He's asking for a wine menu."

"No. We don't have one of those. We do have a chardonnay and a pinot grigio, if you're interested."

Curtis looks at me like he's surprised. "I guess we're drinking cheap tonight." He then looks at Morgan. "I'll have a glass of the chardonnay, and a glass of water with lemon. Two slices, if you can."

"Sure." She casts me a sympathetic smile. "I'll be back for your order in just a minute."

"Take your time," Curtis says, picking up a menu. "We're in no rush."

My eyes meet Morgan's in a silent plea not to do that. She gives me a slight nod and hightails it to the kitchen.

I pick up a menu, too, and try to shake my discomfort. *I'm already here, and I agreed to this. Make the best of it, Ror.*

"So what did you do today?" I ask.

"I had one hell of a day. My ex-wife called. We've been divorced for five years, and she still calls me to come over and fix the air conditioner. I should tell the bitch no, but I don't. You'd think she'd figure out how to use a thermostat by now." He sighs haughtily. "But, like they say, you can't teach an old dog new tricks."

I don't know his ex-wife, but I instinctively feel the need to defend her.

"Growing up, we had a thermostat that never worked right," I say.

"My mother could never get it to kick on. My father always had to do it. It was a joke around the house. It only liked Dad."

"Electronic things typically prefer men."

"Excuse me?" I ask, my eyes widening.

"It's not women's fault. I think it's something in their body chemistry that does it."

I set my menu down, my blood heating. "You know, Curtis, I'm picking up a chauvinistic vibe here, and I should point out before we get too far into this that I'm not the one."

"Here is your chardonnay and your water with two slices of lemon," Morgan says, placing the drinks on the edge of the table. "Would you like to start with an appetizer or jump right into your entrées?"

"Double cheeseburger for me," Curtis says. "Fries are fine on the side."

He hands her his menu.

I haven't even perused mine. But the thought of eating anything right now makes me ill. And I just want to get the hell out of here.

"Same for me," I say, forking over my menu, too. "Thank you, Morgan."

"You're welcome."

She's not two steps away before Curtis lets loose on a tangent about classic cars. Out of nowhere, and with no attempt at finding a topic that I know anything about or have any interest in, for that matter, he goes off about torque. Pistons. Crank shafts, which I gather is not what it sounds like.

I nod here and there, but there's no input needed from me. This is a one-person conversation. I'm just here as a spectator.

I shouldn't be here. I'm not sure what I was thinking agreeing to this farce.

As he chatters away, my thoughts drift to Tate.

*"And to think that my goal has been trying to run into you all day. This doesn't bother you, does it? Me being in your office? Because, if it does, I'll go."*

## The Situation

My heart tugs in my chest.

I've been unfair to him. I've been unfair to *myself*.

Somewhere along the line, I've allowed the monologue in my head to skew to the negative. Instead of looking at a situation and seeing the positive—*what happens if this is the best thing to ever happen to me?*—my mind always goes to the dark side—*what happens if I screw this up and ruin everything?* I don't feel hopeful; I'm fearful. I don't imagine the joy that could come out of something. I go immediately to the potential pain and heartbreak or judge myself preemptively.

I look up at Curtis. His lips are still moving. I watch him jabber on, having muted him in my head, and ask myself what I'm getting out of this. The answer: nothing. So why was I so willing to take this risk when I could've taken a much safer gamble and had dinner with Tate?

*I need to talk to him.*

Adrenaline fires through me, and my eyes dart around for an escape plan. Just as my hand locks around my phone, Morgan appears with our plates. Curtis finally stops jabbering long enough for me to catch my breath.

"Your burgers are here," she says, setting our plates in front of us. "Do you need anything else? Ketchup? Refills?"

*Earplugs.*

"I'll take another chardonnay," Curtis says.

"Could you bring the check whenever you have time?" I ask. "Just to save you the trouble later."

She nods knowingly. "I'll grab that for you. And the chardonnay."

"Ah, dammit," Curtis says, pulling his phone from his shirt pocket. "This is Cathy." He glances up at me. "The ex-wife. Mind if I take this?"

*God bless Cathy.*

"Be my guest," I say, scooting to the edge of the booth. "I'm going to use the ladies' room."

I'm not sure he even hears me.

"I told you I was on a date," he says, smirking. "What do you want?"

*A lobotomy if she's still calling you.*

I speed walk to the restroom, desperate to be alone. I don't have Tate's number and I'm not sure how to get it. *Would Tally have it, by any chance?*

My hand wraps around the door handle, and I twist and push.

As I take a step inside the small room, a palm splays against the small of my back and ushers me inside.

I gasp, swinging around like a madwoman, ready to brawl. But I don't even get turned all the way before I'm hauled into a wide, strong body, and a mouth that I'm very familiar with comes crashing down onto mine.

Tate yanks me to him, carrying us both into the restroom and locking the door behind us.

My brain misfires. It's unable to compute a thought. Instead, my body takes over and I melt into the man I've been thinking about all day.

"What are you doing here?" I ask, my head spinning.

He smirks. "Checking out my competition."

"You really do have stalker tendencies."

He chuckles, pressing another long, leisurely kiss against my lips.

"Maybe," he whispers, cupping my face with his hands. "But I had to know for sure."

"You had to know what?"

His hands slide to the small of my back. "I had to know if I'm crazy to think that we belong together."

My knees wobble, but I'm not in fear of falling. He's holding onto me as if his life depends on it.

I grin at him. "Did you come up with any conclusions?"

"A few."

"Like what?" I ask, toying with the hair at the nape of his neck.

"You look miserable out there."

*The Situation*

I laugh, my chest bouncing against his. "Is it that obvious?"

"I think the fuckhead you're having dinner with is the only one who's oblivious to it."

"Fuckhead?" I laugh. "You don't even know him."

He stares at me. "I'd want to fight him for being with my girl if he wasn't so pathetic."

Fire spreads through me, pooling in my core. The heat in his eyes does nothing to squash it, either.

"Your girl, huh?" I ask, grinning.

"When are you going to stop this and just admit it?"

I hesitate, giving myself a moment to change my mind. This is against the rules I set up for myself months ago. *But am I even the same woman I was then?*

Tate slides his hands beneath my dress and palms my ass cheeks.

*I'm definitely not her.*

"When am I going to admit it?" I ask, smiling smugly at him. "Right. About. Now."

"It's about fucking time."

I lift onto my toes, and he meets me in the middle. His tongue sweeps past my lips like it owns them.

I moan, sagging into him, afraid of what'll happen when he stops.

"God, I missed this," he says, pressing kisses along my jaw and down into the crook of my neck.

"You have no idea." I palm his cock through his pants. He flexes against my hand, emitting a growl that needles my libido. "Or, maybe you do."

His hands travel around the curves of my hips, around my waist, and then slide back to the globes of my ass again. His touch erases all sense from my brain. He now controls my body. I'm officially his, and it's pointless to say otherwise.

"This ass is unbelievable," he says, kissing me again.

My nails dig into his back. "I was coming in here to call you."

"Liar."

"I mean it," I say, bending my head to give him access to my neck. With every lick, kiss, and suck, a band inside me is stretched thinner.

"What were you going to say?"

"I was going to ask you to meet me."

He balls my dress at my waist. "For what?"

He pulls back and looks me in the eye. The intensity makes me shiver.

"I was going to tell you I'm sorry," I whisper.

"For what?"

"For not being honest."

His eyes narrow. "Have you been lying to me?"

I push forward, grazing his groin with my body. His jaw pulses, but he doesn't look away.

"Every time I've said I'm not already yours was a lie," I say.

He lifts me off my feet and sets me on the counter in one fluid motion. His lips find mine. Gone are the kisses born from a need to get off. These are different. These are conversation.

My lip is pulled between his teeth, and the friction makes me moan. His hand slips between my thighs.

I spread my legs for him. The back of my head rests against the mirror behind me.

"Let's see if you're wet," he whispers against my mouth.

"If you touch me, you better be ready to make me come."

He laughs, nipping my lip again. "I've missed this little pussy."

"Now's a perfect time to get reacquainted."

"Fuck, Aurora," he hisses, sliding a finger through my soaked flesh.

I pull his face back to mine and grind myself against his hand. His knuckle bumps my swollen clit, and I moan into Tate's mouth.

"This is all for me," he says, inserting one finger deep inside me.

I close my eyes, absorbing the sweet fire shooting through me.

This is the woman I want to be—beautiful, safe, and respected, but on the verge of being ravaged at any moment.

"I'm going to make you come on my hand," he whispers in my ear. "And you aren't going to yell."

I whimper as he adds a second, then a third finger.

"If you yell, I stop," he warns.

"*Don't stop.*"

"Be good and give me all of your pleasure," he says against the shell of my ear. "Show me that this is mine."

"Is there any way it's not? *Fuck.*" I hold his shoulders as I begin to shake. I'm desperate to finish. "I'm so close."

"Don't. Scream."

He presses on my clit as he strokes the spot inside me that makes it impossible to hold on any longer. The onslaught is quick and fierce, akin to lava pouring through my veins.

"Ah!" I start to yell, but Tate clamps a hand over my mouth.

He stares into my eyes, wickedly amused, as I grind out my orgasm on his hand.

Tears dot the corners of my eyes from the intensity of the moment.

"Shh," he whispers, pulling his hand away and replacing it with his mouth.

Slowly, he guides me back to the real world as the final waves of my climax ripple through me. Tate's kisses turn gentle. His touches turn softer. There's a tenderness to him that is more intoxicating than the passion from moments ago.

"There you go," he says, slipping his fingers out of me. "How was that?"

I try to answer him, but the words are jumbled. I lean against the mirror with my eyes closed.

He chuckles and turns on the tap beside me. I hear the paper towel dispenser activating. Then the tap turns off.

"Spread your legs again for me, gorgeous."

He tenderly runs the damp towels between my legs, cleaning up the mess he just made. There's something so intimate, so sweet about the moment that I find it hard to breathe.

"Hop down for me," he says, helping me to my feet.

"Now what?" I ask, wondering what happens at this point. *Do we walk out together? Do I tell Curtis that I had an emergency?* I have no idea. "This is unchartered territory for me."

"What happens now?" He smiles sinfully. "Now you go back out there and think about how hard you just came while you have your burger with that dipshit."

I gasp. "You expect me to go out there and finish dinner?"

"Hey, you're the one who thought this was a great idea."

I cross my arms over my chest. "It doesn't bother you that I'm on a date with someone else."

"Make no mistake—I hate it." He lifts a brow. "But your body and I seem to have a good rapport. I don't think I have anything to worry about."

"You're terrible."

"Me? You're the one who just got off in a public bathroom while on a date with someone else."

"Don't try to shame me!"

He laughs, pulling me into his chest once again. It's my new favorite place to be. "Shame you? For what? Doing what you should've been doing all along?" He kisses me sweetly. "Let this dinner remind you that no one can take care of you like I can."

*I already know.*

Tate yanks the door open and pats me on the ass. "Have fun at dinner." Then he strolls out casually, leaving me alone.

*That fucker.*

I straighten my dress and fix my hair, taking in my reflection in the mirror. *Rosy cheeks. Glassy eyes. Swollen lips.* There's no fixing this.

A few more people are in the dining area as I make my way back to Curtis.

"Sorry about that," I say, taking my seat.

I glance down at the table, and his plate is empty.

*The Situation*

"Was I gone that long?" I ask, my cheeks heating.

"Nah, I'm a fast eater. And Cathy needs me to come by and check her pipes."

*Cathy, you're a lifesaver.*

"Don't let me keep you," I say a little too happily. "Clogged pipes can be a disaster."

"It's always something with that woman."

He looks away, but I can see the corner of his dimples shine in his cheeks.

"Curtis?" I ask.

"Yeah?"

"It might not be about the thermostat or the clogged pipes, you know."

The semi-scowl on his face all evening begins to fade.

"Maybe listen to her a little bit," I say gently. "She wouldn't be calling you if she didn't still love you."

His eyes brighten almost immediately. "You think so?"

"Yeah. I think so."

He scoots to the edge of the booth. "I've already paid the bill, so as soon as you're done ..."

I consider mentioning that he shouldn't be a chauvinist pig, but decide I've fought enough battles for one day.

My phone lights up with a text from a number I don't recognize. My heart skips a beat.

> Unknown: By the way, you look beautiful tonight.

I laugh, certain my eyes are brighter now, too.

"Come to think of it, I'm not that hungry," I say, reaching for my purse.

"Really?"

I nod. "Really."

Curtis and I walk out side by side. Suddenly, in the strangest way, I'm grateful to him.

The world works in mysterious ways.

# Chapter Nineteen

## Aurora

I get inside my car and start it. Then I pull out my phone and eagerly open my text app.

> Unknown: By the way, you look beautiful tonight.

A grin splits my cheeks as I re-read his message.

> Me: We need to talk.

> Tate: Whenever you're ready.

> Me: You busy for the rest of the night?

His response comes in immediately.

> Tate: I hope so. I have plans with my girl if she can wrap up her date. 🙄

I laugh as my chest swells. *My girl.* I'll never tire of that.

> Me: My date just decided that he needs to check on his ex-wife.

> Tate: You're serious?

> Me: I don't think I was giving "available vibes." But I also think he's still in love with her.

> Tate: Have you left yet?

> Me: Parking lot of the restaurant.

I look up as a firetruck rushes by. The sirens wail so loud that my rearview mirror rattles. Wow.

> Tate: Dropped Pin [Map Thumbnail of the pinned location] 72961 Annabella Drive, Nashville, TN

> Me: What's this?

> Tate: My address. Meet me there.

> Me: I get your phone number and your address in the same night? 😏

> Tate: Do you think that's all you're getting? 😼

*The Situation*

I stare at his words, unsure what he means. They could be taken many ways. But after what just happened in the restroom, I'm willing to bet I'm going to like it. A lot.

Instead of asking him for clarification, I put his address into my navigation system.

> Me: I can be there in 26 minutes.

> Tate: I'll be waiting.

# Chapter Twenty

## Aurora

"What the heck is this?" I mutter.

I hit the brakes and slow roll to what appears to be a guard shack in front of two large metal gates. A man slides open a window as I roll mine down. He peers into the car as if I'm transporting illegal substances.

*Perhaps I was put on a watch list, after all.*

"Hi," I say, though it's more of a question than a greeting.

"Good evening. Your name, please."

"Aurora Johnson. I'm here to see Tate Brewer."

He lifts his collar to his mouth, pauses, and then turns back to me. The gates slowly swing open.

"Enjoy your evening, Ms. Johnson," he says.

"Thanks."

*The Situation*

I roll up my window and proceed down the driveway, taking the bends and curves, until the forest on both sides finally cuts away.

*Holy hell.*

Jamie pointed out that Tate was a billionaire, but I didn't give it much thought. That might've been a mistake because the house standing in front of me is the kind of place you see on an architectural show of award-winning designs.

The last rays of sunlight streak through the sky behind the towering structure. A blend of brick, wood, and stucco marries seamlessly on the facade, and a long porch stretches along most of the front. All that's missing is a porch swing—and maybe a dog.

I survey the scene and try to decide where to park. There's the front door, but there's also an open garage door on the side of the house. I have no idea which one I'm supposed to use.

Making an executive decision, I park at the end of the sidewalk leading to the porch.

I turn the car off and get out, locking it behind me. My heart pounds harder with each step I take up the walkway. There's no going back from this. If I go inside his home, things between us go from being a version of fuck buddies to something more real.

I gulp.

Just as I get to the bottom of the steps, the front door opens, and all of my nerves disappear.

Tate stands in the doorway with his shirt unbuttoned. His hair is messy from having my hands in it. He flashes me a bright, easy smile —the kind of smile that you see on people in advertisements where they're pretending to be happy.

Only, this isn't an ad.

"You found it," he says, holding his arms wide.

I nearly jog up the remaining steps and launch myself into his chest. "What do you mean I found it? It's impossible to miss."

He wraps me up and holds me close, pressing a kiss to the top of my head.

"You got here fast," he says, leading me inside. He puts my keys on a small wooden table by the door. "I got here about ten minutes ago."

"Traffic was light."

He grins, knowing damn good and well that I raced over here like a bat out of hell.

"Welcome to my humble abode," he says.

I take a step back and gasp. "Oh wow, Tate. This is beautiful."

"It's okay."

My eyeballs nearly pop out of my head. "*It's okay?* Are you serious? This is stunning."

"I like it. It's pretty clean and natural, for the most part. Low maintenance."

"So what you're saying is that you don't go from room to room and change everything every six months?"

He laughs. "I've lived here for five years, and I just managed to fill the last room with furniture a few months ago."

I look at him in disbelief. *This is a dream home. How can he be so nonchalant about it?*

*Oh, right. He's a billionaire.*

"Would you like a drink?" he asks. "Water? Soda? Wine? I might have a beer somewhere."

"A water would be great." I glance down at his bare feet. "Should I take my shoes off? I don't know if that seems presumptuous or if it's good manners?"

He flashes me a killer smile. "You're here. That's all I care about."

Tate walks barefoot into the kitchen, leaving me swooning behind. I hurriedly kick off my shoes, then follow him through an arched doorway.

"I hope you cook in here because this kitchen was made for meal prep," I say, trying not to let my jaw sweep the floor.

If the entryway was stunning, I'm not sure what to call the kitchen. The cabinets are the same color as the wood floors, and the appliances blend in. I have no clue where the fridge or dishwasher are. The counters are a pristine white stone with light gray and gold

## The Situation

veins. A deep farmhouse sink centered on a wide window runs nearly the whole length of the counter. The view from the glass is all fields, forests, and the city skyline off in the distance.

A window seat is built into a smaller window beside the island, and I can imagine curling up there with a book on a rainy day.

"What are you thinking?" he asks.

I sit on a barstool at the island, watching him pour me a glass of water.

"I'm thinking that this space is perfect for big holiday dinners, and late nights with cocktails or cookies and milk while sharing stories and dreams."

"Sounds nice. Let's try it sometime."

My heart flutters.

"I was afraid your security guy wasn't going to let me in," I say. "He's pretty serious."

"Ah, they all are while they're new. He's not been around too long."

"Do you always have security?"

He nods, handing me a glass. "Yeah. I've cut mine back to the guard shack at the front, and one guy who roams the property. I only keep him for my mother's well-being."

"That's nice of you."

"She's been through enough. It's a small thing to me, but a big thing for her."

He casually takes a drink as if every twenty-seven-year-old man is keen on making his mother's life easier.

"Are you and your mother close?" I ask.

"I mean, that's complicated. I guess we are. I talk to her a couple of times a week, and I'm her favorite, naturally."

"Oh, of course." I grin. "I think it's sweet that you have such a good relationship."

"She's been through a lot. Our father put her through hell."

His features harden, and a fire flashes in his eyes. The kind, sweet Tate I've grown to know is momentarily gone.

"I assume you know that story," he says, his voice cool and tight.

I shake my head.

"It was all over the news a few years ago." His chest rises and falls slowly. "The quick and dirty is that my father is currently in prison for a lot of shit, including money laundering, attempted murder for trying to kill my sister—"

I gasp.

"—and conspiracy to commit murder thanks to the hitman he hired to kill Mom."

My eyeballs nearly pop out of my head.

He watches my reaction. His beautiful body is rigid. It takes me a long moment to realize that he's putting up his guard—that he expects there's a chance that I'll look at him differently now that I know about his father.

I get up from my seat and move around the island. He watches me warily each step of the way.

My arms wrap around his waist, and I bury my head in his chest. He stills before he relents. I'm enveloped in the biggest, tightest hug of my entire life.

"I'm sorry that happened to you," I say. "And to your mother, and the rest of your family."

He nestles his face in my hair.

We stand like this in the middle of his kitchen for the longest time, well past the moment the sun settles beyond the horizon. No words are exchanged. None are needed.

Finally, he gives me one last squeeze and steps back. His eyes are hesitant, like he's unsure where I'll take this conversation.

"Do you want to talk about it?" I ask.

"Nope."

"Then how did you find me tonight?"

A slow ripple of relief flows across his features, and he exhales.

"Tally," he says.

"Tally?" I laugh. "You're joking."

He smirks. "I don't think she meant to tell me."

I narrow my eyes, trying to decide whether I believe that or not. He *is* her boss's boss, so, on one hand, I could understand her answering him truthfully if he asked. But I can also see her being so dazzled by him that she just forked over the information without realizing it.

Tate can be a persuasive beast. And, well, it worked out for me, anyway.

I pick up my glass. "I'll forgive her. I remember what it's like to be young and easily impressed."

"What were you like when you were her age?"

"At her age? Well, let's see … I probably would've been a cheerleader for a pro football team and wrapping up college."

"You were a cheerleader?"

I nod.

"Did I know that?" he asks.

"I don't know. I haven't told you, but you always have a way of knowing shit." I shrug. "That experience helps me in putting together the team for the Raptors. We had a great team in Chicago, and I learned a lot about what makes a group effective and what doesn't."

"Makes sense."

He opens a cabinet, which happens to be the fridge, and pulls out a plate. He places it on the island, grinning.

A blueberry pie—not as pretty or perfect as the one from Ruma, but it looks delicious nonetheless, and shines from a pale pink pie plate.

"Where'd you get that?" I ask, laughing.

"Someone stole a whole pie from me, so I had to make one myself."

I grin. "*You* made that?"

"I sure did."

"*Tate.*"

"*What?*" He beams proudly. "Flour, salt, sugar, very cold and unsalted butter, and ice water. That's it. Pretty simple."

My mouth hangs agape.

"Mimi taught me," he says. "Wednesday is our date night, so I was seeing her right before I saw you." He sighs dramatically. "It's hard keeping up with two women."

"And you made that pie?"

"You don't believe me?" He demonstrates how he crimps the edges. "We make something sweet every week, and she sends most of it home with me. That's probably why I haven't been posting shirtless selfies much anymore. I'm starting to pack on the pounds."

I snort, rolling my eyes. "Stop it."

"Mimi sends me home with pie. You stole my pie."

"Mimi sends you home with pie," I say, feathering my lips over his. "I sent you home with ... me."

He takes my hand and puts it on his cock.

"You never fail to impress," I say, my nipples hardening.

"Now that I have you here, I might just keep you."

Thoughts of him tying me up come roaring back through my brain. "I might go along with that, depending on the circumstances."

He pulls back, surprised.

"I was kidding," I say, smacking his chest with the hand that isn't massaging his balls through his pants.

"I'm not." He drags his tongue along my bottom lip. "I'm all in."

"You can't be all in," I say, pulling back just before he nips my jaw. "We just met."

"That's unfortunate, isn't it?"

"What's unfortunate?" I gasp a breath as he sucks gently on the spot my shoulder meets my neck.

"That we just met."

"If it were too much earlier than now, you would've been underage."

He blows across the dampened skin. "Shut up."

"It's true." Goose bumps flare down my arms. "Our age gap doesn't bother you?"

He stands, rolling his eyes, irritated with me. "No. It doesn't. If

## The Situation

anything, it makes it hotter. If I wanted someone younger, I'd get one. And if I wanted someone more beautiful ..."

I hold my breath, bracing myself for whatever he's about to say.

He leans in and kisses me. "I'd never find anyone."

He peers into my eyes, letting me see all of him. There's no shield, no games—there's nothing but raw, genuineness reflected at me.

I'm done. I'm done questioning this. I'm done asking if it's real, if it's too soon, or why it's happening at all.

I've been on a quest to do the right thing and create a life I love. But if I stop being myself, if I stop trusting my gut—am I simply pretending to be someone I'm not?

Because Aurora Johnson is a romantic. I follow my heart. It might not always work out for me, but does anything ever work out every time?

If I want to live my whole truth, I need to lean into the pillars that make me who I am. That includes falling in love, no matter the circumstances.

A slow smile slips across my face as the trepidation I've lived with washes away. In its place is relief ... and a tingling in my chest.

"Come here," I say, pulling him to me.

I don't know what's come over me, but I'm not fighting it—or him, anymore.

# Chapter Twenty-One

## Tate

Aurora grabs the waistband of my pants and drags me to her.

Blood hammers in my ears as she undoes my belt and then the button on my fly. She looks up at me through her thick lashes and slowly pulls the belt from around my middle. It snaps as it frees and hits the floor.

Her grin is coy. *She knows what she's doing to me.*

"I want to fuck you," I say, my breath hot. Every move she makes causes her knuckles to brush against my bulge. As much as I like to think I have self-restraint, I can't seem to find it tonight.

She shakes her head.

"What do you mean *no*?" I ask.

"Be patient."

*Be patient, my ass.* I yank my shirt off and toss it onto the counter.

## The Situation

Her palms waste no time finding my bare skin, exploring the ridges and valleys of my abs.

Her touch is like bolts of thunder echoing through my body. I shiver, clenching my hands so I don't grab her and sink my dick into that sweet little pussy.

She steps back, teasing me—bending over to gather the hem of her dress. The view of the tops of her tits is unobstructed, and I want to feel them in my hands. In my mouth. Pressed against my torso as she comes.

My cock pushes against its constraints, the head already swollen for her.

"It's getting hot in here, isn't it?" she asks coyly before dragging the pale yellow material over her head.

Inch by inch, her body is exposed. Soft curves. Delicate dips. Round edges. *Pure perfection.*

"I've jacked off to the idea of you so many times," I say, watching her turn in a circle for me. "And, to think, you were real all of this time."

"Is there anyone here?" she asks. "Can the security guys see inside the house?"

"No."

"Zero chance?"

"Negative two."

She smirks, taking my hand in hers. "Good."

"Where are we going?"

Not that I really care. *She's naked.* I'd listen to Gannon talk about investments all night if I got to look at her.

She climbs up into the window seat that I've never once used, her ass jiggling as she crawls to the back.

The moon is bright in the dark sky behind her. It illuminates her, making the air around her glow as she works to position three pillows to her liking. I adjust myself, wincing as the pain of needing to shed these pants almost becomes too much.

"Okay," she says, sitting on her knees. "Come on."

I climb in beside her, resting my back against the pillows. My breath hitches in my throat as Aurora straddles me.

"Damn," I hiss, making sure my zipper is tucked away so it doesn't hurt her. As I withdraw my fingers, they slide against her clit, making her shiver. "You're ready for me again, aren't you?"

Her eyes blaze as she rests her pussy on my lap.

She throws her arms over my shoulders and brings her mouth to mine. Slowly, her hips start to move.

"Fuck," I mutter against her lips.

She whimpers into my mouth, and I swallow her sweet, soft sounds.

I flex my hips, giving her a better angle to grind against. She rocks against me, rolling her hips to get the best friction against her clit.

"Do you like this?" I ask, eager to learn her favorite *everything*.

"I like everything with you."

Her words are breathless, so soft they're nearly unable to be heard. She closes her eyes and tilts her head back, soaking my pants as she moves harder.

I cup her tits, bringing one nipple to my mouth. As soon as my tongue touches her swollen bud, she moans.

My cock pulses, balls tightening so hard it aches.

I suck her into my mouth, rolling the flat part of my tongue around the peak.

Her knees spread farther, lowering her even heavier onto my lap. I drop my hands to her ass, squeezing her cheeks until she yelps in a mixture of pleasure and pain.

"Tate," she says, her pitch rising.

Her movements become more deliberate. Faster. *Harder*. I thrust against her, wanting to give her what she wants.

She's so beautiful riding me this way and knowing that she's relaxed enough with me to try something like this—that I'm a safe place for her to explore—makes me even harder.

Closer to losing control.

*Hold it. Hold it. Don't you blow, you fucker.*

## The Situation

Sweat gathers on my forehead as I catch her scent filling the air. Her wetness coats the tips of my fingers. The heat of her pussy against my cock intensifies as she grinds down on it.

"I gotta stop," I say, trying to make her still.

"No, don't. *Please*."

*Dammit.*

Her tits bounce as she arches her back. I grit my teeth, trying to think about something else. *Anything else*—something to put some distance between this little minx and the cum threatening to spill from my cock. But her little moans as she starts to climax make it impossible not to be in the moment.

*I want to be here.* I don't want to miss a motherfucking thing.

Her head falls forward, and I capture her mouth with mine. It's nearly as hot and wet as her pussy. My tongue glides against hers, coaxing her to relax and fall apart—to come on me.

I grab the back of her hair and tug. Her mouth leaves mine as she yelps, and I bend forward and bury my face in those perfect, teardrop-shaped tits.

My fingers dip into her ass, encouraging her to grind, before moving to her hips and pushing her down on me.

"Tate!" She yells my name as her body begins to shake, and her juices soak through my pants and slick my cock.

That's the match that makes this explosion instantaneous ... and uncontrollable.

"*Fuck*," I groan, shuddering as heat shoots through my groin.

It's too late to stop it, even if I wanted to.

She bucks against me, riding out her orgasm. I meet her thrust for thrust, working through mine.

My lap is soaked and sticky, and my skin is covered in sweat.

And the most beautiful woman I've ever seen is staring at me with a twinkle in her eyes.

For a moment, we just watch each other. Then, together, we start to laugh.

She falls against my chest, resting her head against my shoulder. I wrap my arms around her and hold her close.

"I have to admit," I say, my face flushing. "This is a first for me."

"Yay!" She giggles, pulling back. She cups my face in her hands. "I don't know how you feel about that."

"Slightly embarrassed."

She kisses the tip of my nose. "Don't be. I'm going to be thinking about the fact that I made the great Tate Brewer come in his pants for years."

I smack her ass just hard enough for it to crack.

"Hey!" She laughs again. "That was great. I needed that."

"I'm glad."

"But now I need something else."

I brush her hair out of her face. "What's that?"

"A piece of pie."

"And here I thought you were going to ask to ride my face."

Her eyes darken. "That'll be dessert."

"I thought pie was dessert?"

"You thought wrong."

She lifts off me and climbs out of the window seat. I don't dare look at my groin. And thankfully, Aurora doesn't comment about it, either.

"Want to grab a shower?" I ask.

"Can I take one with you?"

I laugh, picking her up, letting her legs dangle over my arms. "Like there was another option."

She kisses me all the way to the bathroom.

## Chapter Twenty-Two

# A urora

"It hit me straight in the forehead," Tate says, mimicking getting smacked in the face with a hockey puck. "That was the last day I got on the ice."

I laugh at the look of horror on his face as he relives the memory.

"It traumatized you, didn't it?" I ask.

"Have you ever been hit in the face with something hard and ..." He smirks. "Never mind."

I elbow him in the stomach, making him chuckle.

We've been tucked away naked in his bedroom for hours. I left once to pee. He left one time to grab water and pie for us. Otherwise, Wednesday faded into Thursday with a soundtrack of our laughter.

My leg drapes over Tate's. His hand rests on my thigh, gently stroking it back and forth. I'm not sure he even realizes he's doing it at this point.

And I love it.

"Can't be too mad at hockey, though," he says. "It brought me to you."

I slide my fork into the pie we've so carefully positioned on a pillow between us. "What are you going to do if Charlie comes back?"

It's a thought that's run through my mind a few times tonight during our haphazard conversations. *Will he go back to traveling? Work out of another office? Stay at the Raptors?*

"What would you like me to do?" he asks.

"It's not really my choice."

"Maybe it's not ultimately your choice, but you have a say in the matter."

I look at him, both brows lifted. "This is business. Your family counts on you. What I think doesn't matter."

He falls deeper into the pillows and shakes his head as if something I said amuses and frustrates him at the same time.

"What?" I ask, shoving the bite of pie in my mouth.

"Nothing."

"No, *what?*"

"You don't want to hear it," he says, staring at the ceiling.

"I don't want to hear half of the things you say, but I listen."

He turns to me, dropping his jaw for my benefit.

I laugh. "Really. Tell me what you were thinking."

"You can only blame yourself for this."

"Sounds about right."

He rolls his eyes. "When McCabe comes back, or when we find a replacement for him, I need to do something conducive to the rest of my life."

I shrug, taking another bite. "Of course."

"And you, gorgeous, are a part of the rest of my life."

My chest tightens. The fork nearly falls out of my hand.

"You made me say it," he says. "I wasn't going to go there."

## The Situation

I lay the utensil back in the pan. When I look at him, he's smiling as if we're still talking about an errant hockey puck twenty years ago.

His words both scare and comfort me. I can't help but wonder if those emotions are not two sides of the same coin. *Is it possible to feel comfortable if you haven't identified and moved past the things that scare you?*

I don't know how to respond to him, so I change the subject.

"The Good Day reports were emailed to me this evening," I say. "I took a quick look at them before I left my house for Caesar's. Interesting stuff. Derek will tear into those numbers tomorrow and regurgitate them to the rest of us by the beginning of next week. I copied Charlie on it, just in case."

"How do you feel about the rebrand?" he asks.

"I think the team has done an excellent job so far. Tally has been identifying community outreach projects we can get involved with, and I must admit, I'm surprised it hasn't been done with the team before. We have lots of things in the works not to just appeal to your typical male hockey fan demographic, but to bring in women and children, too."

He smiles. "I love the way you light up when you talk shop."

*I do?*

"Your body is fucking fire, but your brain is the sexiest thing about you," he says. "And I mean that in the best way."

"*Wow*. I don't think anyone has ever complimented my brain before."

"Have you always worked in sports marketing?"

I laugh, finding the question amusing. "No. This is the first time I've worked directly in a marketing position like this."

"No shit?"

"Like I said, I worked as a cheerleader for a while in my twenties. That's essentially marketing. But I did that just to be involved with sports because I loved them so much but could never play." I paste on a fake smile. "Little girls don't get dirty."

He draws a line up my leg to the apex of my thighs. "Your parents would be very disappointed in you tonight."

"You have no clue. I didn't have sex until I married my first husband, and, in retrospect, I probably only married him so I could have sex. He was a virgin, too."

Tate's hand stops moving. "Kudos to him for waiting ... but how?"

"He went to our church."

"That's some kind of dedication."

He pulls his arm back and picks up his fork.

"There was no dedication in that marriage," I say, stretching and yawning. "Neither of them, really. Not to me, anyway. The first one had control issues. I see that now. He had a love/hate relationship with me working for the Legends. He supported me publicly but shamed me at home. Actually, he took a job here in Nashville, so I'd have to quit."

"What a fuck."

"It gets better," I say, laughing angrily. "He told me he didn't want to have kids about a year into our marriage—knowing I did. But we were already married, and I thought maybe he'd come around. He did." I shake my head. "He went on a mission trip and came home with a pregnant mistress."

*"Holy shit."* Tate's eyes widen. "You're kidding me."

"Nope. That's why I divorced him. Now, my second husband was the opposite. He was obsessed with me, I think. I know that sounds amazing."

My stomach tightens, and I almost don't finish the story. But with every sentence I say, a bit more of the heaviness I carry around is lifted from my chest.

Tate stills. "What happened with him?"

I force a swallow. "Two things were the nails in his coffin. First, his daughter was coming over for dinner, and I had forgotten to put the meat out to thaw the night before. So that morning, I ran to the grocery to buy a pot roast." My stomach churns. "He happened to have swung by the house while I was gone and was furious that I'd gone to the store alone. I don't think he believed me. I think he thought I was with someone else, maybe."

Tate's fork hits the pan with a *clink*.

"She came over that night, and I had to create a lie to explain why my back was stiff and bruised."

I barely get the words out before Tate pulls me into his chest. He holds me so tightly that I can scarcely breathe. And when I realize that no one has ever held me like this in my entire life before now, tears slip down my cheeks.

"Where is he now?" he asks, his voice rough.

"Far away from here. His daughter's husband took care of it, and I never got the chance to really thank him." I press a kiss to his sternum before lifting and wiping my cheeks with the sheet. "What about you? Have you been married? Engaged?"

He looks at me warily, as if he hasn't gotten past my admission. I shake my head, silently telling him that I need to move this conversation along. And because he somehow understands me already, he acquiesces even though I know he doesn't want to.

He clears his throat. "I have not been married or engaged."

"That surprises me."

"Why?"

I shrug. "I can imagine lines of women throwing themselves at you."

"Well, they do. That's true."

I snort-laugh.

He grins, and the light slowly filters back in his eyes. "My parents fought my whole life. Well, they didn't really fight in front of us. It was just obvious, to me at least, they didn't like each other."

"That's sad."

"I've always known that I wanted to have a family, have a home. I've wanted a beautiful wife and a house that smells like pie."

*That's the sweetest thing I've ever heard.*

He reaches for my hand and laces our fingers together.

"I've always said that I'm going to do it once—find the right girl and sweep her off her feet," he says, monitoring my reaction.

I don't give him one—not one that he can use.

"Yeah, well, I thought that too, and I married two of the wrong ones," I say. "It doesn't always work out like that."

"Guess I'm a better judge of character than you."

"Fuck off," I say, laughing.

"Hey, when you know, you know." He shrugs. "That's what my brothers have told me, and I didn't think Gannon would ever be happy."

I scooch around so I'm facing him. He appears to prefer this position. His hands slide right into my lap. *I prefer this position, too.*

"Was Gannon who you were talking about in Nashville? The one you called a prick? The asshole boss?"

Tate snickers. "Yup."

"That's mean!"

"He *is* a prick sometimes," he says. "But he married my best friend, which is great for him and terrible for me because I lost her in the deal. But they're happy, and I still call Carys whenever I want to—"

"*Wait.*" My jaw drops. *No. This is not ... no.* "What's her name?"

"Carys," he says slowly.

*Oh God.* I close my eyes. "What's her last name, Tate?"

"Johnso ... *holy fuck.*"

*Holy fuck is right.*

He shoots up in bed.

Cringing, I open my eyes and brace myself.

My features display shock, in that my ex-stepdaughter is my ... whatever Tate is to me at this point's best friend. Tate's features also display shock in a much more entertaining way.

*This is not going to be good.*

"You're the hot stepmommy," he says, his eyes twinkling.

"What are you talking about?"

He climbs out of bed, laughing hysterically. "Why didn't I put

## The Situation

this together before now? It all makes sense." He faces me as if he just solved world hunger. "The Legends! That's why that was so familiar to me."

"How did you know that?"

"Carys might've stalked you—don't judge her, though. Never tell her that I told you that."

*She stalked me?* "Okay ..."

"It was harmless," he says. "Don't panic. *Anyway,* I saw a picture of you looking hot as fuck in your cheer uniform. And I've always teased Carys that I wanted to bang her hot stepmommy. *Now I'm banging her hot stepmommy.*"

"Never call me that again."

He cackles. "New kink unlocked."

"Stop it!"

"Wanna role-play?" He wiggles his brows. "You can—"

"Tate! Stop," I say, trying not to laugh at his ridiculousness.

"You didn't even hear me out."

I sigh.

"You can call me Daddy if you want."

I climb out of bed and cross my arms over my chest. "This isn't funny."

He grabs his cock and palms it. "You're right. *It's hot as fuck.*"

Tate walks toward me with a glimmer in his eye. I take a step back. Then another. His smile grows wider with each movement, and the pull in my core grows tighter.

"Don't look at me like that," I say. He opens his mouth, but I can read his mind. "And don't call me Mommy."

He growls, still moving forward. "You're taking the fun out of this."

"What are you doing?" I ask, laughing. My heartbeat picks up. "You're making me nervous."

He leaps forward, and I stumble backward, shrieking as I land on the bed. My ass lands in the pie plate and blueberry pie filling squirts everywhere.

"Tate! Wait!" I say, trying to warn him about the mess.

If he hears me, he pays no attention to it. He's on me before all the syllables fall from my lips.

"Pie," I say, looking at him hovering over me. "Sorry."

He kisses me quickly and then rolls to the side. A sneaky smile graces his lips.

"Don't be sorry," he says, scooping a blob of the filling with his finger. Then he dangles it over my naked chest, letting it fall between my breasts.

My chest rises and falls rapidly. I giggle. "What are you doing?"

"I have to clean up my messes, right, Mo—"

"Tate! Don't you dare ... *ah!*"

His tongue slides down my chest, lapping up the dark blue blob. His eyes stay trained on me as I wiggle beneath him.

His right palm is covered with the dessert, and he plants it just below my belly button. The mixture is sticky and soft. The entire room is perfumed like blueberries. Tate smears the mixture up my torso and my nipples, painting the buds with his fingertips.

"*Oops*," he says, grinning devilishly.

"Right. *Oops,* my ass."

"I can *oops* your ass."

I shriek as he turns me over, smacks my ass, and blueberry pie goes everywhere.

"This is going to stain everything," I say, laughing. "You're nuts!"

He lies next to me, his hand resting on my backside. His smile lights up the room. Somehow, it shines on the inner corners of my heart—the parts that have been hidden in the shadows for far too long.

His kiss is tender and sweet, and I melt into him. But as he pulls away, his smirk is back.

"Ready to get eaten, Stepmommy?"

"Tate!"

His laughter mixes with mine. And if this is the kind of relationship Tate has in mind, I might be okay with it after all.

# Chapter Twenty-Three

T ate

> Me: I need help.

I lean against the bathroom doorframe and watch Aurora sleep. I've never seen someone so peaceful. Not that I've ever watched someone else sleep.

It was hard for me to get out of bed and climb into the shower. *What am I going to do when she wants to go back to her house? How do people handle this?*

*Why won't she just marry me now?*

My screen lights up.

> Astrid: Weird bat call.

> Me: 😐

> Astrid: What do you want?

> Me: About 50 candles delivered to my house, please. I think I like amber and vanilla. Does that sound right?

> Astrid: How in the world would I know what scents you like?

"I should've written that down somewhere," I mumble.

> Me: Go with that. Feel free to wing it with other stuff, too.

I glance up at my blueberry-stained sheets.

> Me: I like blueberry.

> Astrid: I officially know more than I ever wanted to know about you.

> Me: You could sell that information.

> Astrid: Oh my God.

> Me: Can you have someone put them in one of my closets?

> Astrid: Any specific closet?

> Me: Nah. Whatever. 🤖

Aurora moves, the sheets slipping across her body. She's so soft

*The Situation*

and delicate. I just want to protect her—to keep anything bad from ever happening to her. Again.

My jaw clenches as I turn back to my phone.

> **Astrid:** Anything else while I'm doing the most random shit for you today?
>
> **Me:** Yes. Thanks for asking. I need "fuzzy" blankets. Just toss them throughout the house.
>
> **Astrid:** Size? Shape? Colors? Textures?
>
> **Me:** Assorted. Assorted. Assorted but not white. Cozy.
>
> **Astrid:** SO HELPFUL. Due date?
>
> **Me:** Tonight by six-ish?
>
> **Astrid:** I don't get paid enough for this.
>
> **Me:** I'll get you a raise. All you have to do is ask. (I'm not Gannon.)
>
> **Astrid:** Bye, Tate.
>
> **Me:** 🙂

I glance at Aurora one final time, then finish getting ready for work.

## Chapter Twenty-Four

T ate

"How are you feeling?" I ask, finding Carys in the kitchen. She looks tired and paler than usual, but she's upright. That's a good sign. "Sick of soup yet?"

She snarls. "I never want to see a soup again."

I laugh, hopping on a barstool.

"Why are you here midmorning?" she asks, pouring hot water into a tea mug. "Want some tea?"

"No, thanks. I'm here to check on you and Ivy. And I wanted to discuss something with you and Gannon. Is he around?"

"Yeah. He just got out of the shower. He'll be out here in a few."

I glance around Gannon's house and can hardly believe it's the same bachelor pad it used to be. It used to feel cavernous. And blank. It was always cold, too. But now that Carys and baby Ivy are here, it's completely different. There are bright colors and furniture that you can sit on. Pictures and mementos hang on the walls and are propped up on side tables, and baby toys are *everywhere*.

It's a home.

I can't help but wonder how Aurora will change my house, and how many times she'll redecorate it. *What will our kids play with? Will we have a playroom or just let them take over the whole house?*

"Hey, Tate," Gannon says, his hair still wet from the shower. "Didn't know you were here."

"Didn't know you were here either," I say. "Do you ever work anymore?"

Gannon and Carys exchange a look. I feel it in the pit of my stomach.

"What?" I ask, looking between them.

"I guess we might as well start with you," Gannon says.

"The last time someone said that to me, I was in the principal's office."

He takes a mug from Carys and pauses to kiss her. "I've been thinking a lot about businesses, work, and life itself."

"Are you getting philosophical?"

"And I've decided I don't want to do this shit anymore."

*What?* "What shit?"

"All of it." He shrugs. "I don't want to be the head of Brewer Group anymore." He sips his tea, moving around the kitchen. "I don't care about it anymore. Not sure I ever did."

I take a deep breath and let this admission sink into my brain.

I can't say I'm shocked to hear this. Gannon was never the one poised to take over after our father. It was always Bianca. But he stepped into the role after she stepped aside and kept things going while we struggled to keep our heads above water.

Now that we're above deck on everything but the Raptors, I can't blame Gannon for wanting to walk away. I would've done it way before now.

"My blood pressure is going up," Gannon says. "I'm on a pill to lower it now. For what? To keep something alive that is a testament to our father's legacy? Fuck that, and fuck him."

"Amen."

"I want to be here with Carys and Ivy. I don't need to go to work. None of us do. Our kids won't have to work if they don't want to. So why are any of us doing this if it isn't what we want to do?"

Carys watches the back-and-forth from the other side of the island.

"I know why I do it," I say.

"Why?" he asks.

I grin. "Because you do."

He balks.

"Gan, I don't give one flying fuck about Brewer Group, and I couldn't care less about preserving Dad's legacy. What I do care about is *you*, even though you're a prick, and I couldn't let you do it alone."

Carys covers her mouth, but I can still hear her giggle.

"I couldn't abandon you when you were trying to pull it all together for the rest of us. Hell, I knew you didn't want to be doing it from the day Bianca left to go to Florida."

His face softens.

"I respect the hell out of you, brother. And I respect you even more for doing what's right for your family." I glance at Carys and wink before turning back to her husband. "You need to be here, taking care of our girls."

Gannon groans. "You always have to blow it."

I laugh.

"What do you propose we do?" I ask, releasing a breath.

"First, I want to see if any of you want to take the reins at Brewer Group."

"Again, not a hard question to answer." I shift in my seat. "Me? No. If you go, I go. Ripley? I love him, but he's not smart enough to do your job."

*The Situation*

Gannon's lips twitch.

"Jason won't. Bianca will laugh in your face. And Renn will likely pass, but he's the wild card."

"That's about how I see it, too."

I fold my hands on the counter. "So what do you do? Sell it? Because while no one is going to want to spearhead Brewer Group, Renn will want to keep the Royals. Ripley might want the Arrows, although I'm not sure. Jason will keep Brewer Air, but that's not under the umbrella company anyway, so it doesn't matter."

"I've talked to our attorney over the past couple of weeks. We can separate anything we want from the Brewer Group and sell what's left."

"Sounds like a plan to me."

"You're good with this?"

"Fuck, yeah. Want to hop on a group text and settle it now?"

Gannon rolls his eyes. "This isn't the kind of thing you can handle on a group text."

"You just say that because you're old."

I whip my phone out. I have a text sent before Gannon can stop me.

> Me: Hey, fam. Gannon wants to retire. Here are our options—one of you takes over Brewer Group, we sell it all, or sell it all minus whatever you want to keep. Brewer Air is already exempt because Jason wouldn't let Dad incorporate it into BG. (Nerd.)

"Dammit, Tate," Gannon says as his phone goes off.

Carys mouths, *"Thank you,"* from across the room.

"You'll thank me when this is over in ten minutes," I tell my brother as a host of dings break through the air.

I unlock my screen.

> Jason: This NERD had forethought. Whatever you guys decide works for me.
>
> Bianca: It's about damn time. (I don't want anything.)
>
> Renn: Let me talk to Blakely, but we might want to keep the Royals.
>
> Tate: I don't want anything. I never liked working anyway.
>
> Bianca: 🙄
>
> Jason: 😳
>
> Ripley: I see a lot of potential in the Arrows. Let me get back to you.

Gannon looks at me and holds my gaze. He doesn't say thank you, but I know he means it.

> Gannon: Let me know, Renn and Rip. I'll get with the attorneys next week and get this process started.

"You're welcome," I say, locking my screen and shoving my phone in my pocket. "Now that I've solved all of your problems, you can help solve one of mine."

The anger I've battled all night and this morning rears its ugly head.

I grab the collar of my shirt and pull it away from my face. Carys looks toward me with a curious, yet worried look in her eye. She grabs Gannon's arm as she stands next to him, across the counter from me.

"As you know, I met my future wife," I say. "No Kelly jokes. Now isn't the time."

## The Situation

Gannon holds his hands in front of him. "Not saying a word."

"Guess who she is." I pause but can only manage to wait a couple of seconds. "Time's up. Her name is Aurora Johnson."

"Who?" Gannon asks.

Carys's jaw drops. "You're kidding me."

"I'm not. I am, in fact, banging your hot stepmommy."

Gannon's lip twitches. "Only you, Tate. Only you."

"I'm ... shocked," Carys says, looking bewildered. "I haven't talked to her since she called to apologize for how Dad's birthday dinner went and to tell me she was divorcing him."

"Nice segue." I turn to my brother. "Do you know where the motherfucker is?"

"Why?"

"General question."

"That I'm not going to answer as long as you're looking at me like that."

I hop off the stool, unable to sit still any longer. My fingers flex to hit something. My skin is too small for my body. Adrenaline courses through me as I think about Aurora's ex-husband's hands on her.

"Did you know that your father abused Aurora?" I ask, licking my lips.

Carys's eyes widen, and she shakes her head. "No."

"Did he ever touch you?" Gannon asks, his eyes darkening.

"No," she says, shaking her head again. "*No.* Absolutely not."

My brother and I exchange a look. Between the two of us, Kent Johnson's days are numbered.

"Apparently, there was a dinner she was making for you, I think. Pot roast? And—"

"Oh my God. Yes! She had hurt her back somehow. I think she said she fell."

"Yeah, well, your dad did that to her."

Carys covers her mouth. "Is she okay?"

"She's okay. Your dad is a dead man as soon as I get my hands on him."

"Tate," Carys says, "you can't do that. Not because he's my dad. Fuck that. But you can't get in trouble over someone who isn't worth your time."

I glance at Gannon for support. He winks.

"Yeah, Tate," he says, pointedly. "Let's use our heads here."

Ivy's cries ring through the baby monitor propped up on a fruit basket.

"Let me get her," I say, knowing Gannon needs a few minutes alone with his wife.

I head down the hall and open my niece's door. She's sitting in the middle of her bed, sniffling. Her dark hair is wild, sticking everywhere but down.

She's the cutest little thing ever.

"Rough nap, baby girl?" I ask.

She smiles when she sees me. "Ta! Ta!"

"Yeah," I say, chuckling. "Tate. Can you say Tate?"

"Ta!" She reaches for me. "Up."

"You learned a new word, you little smartie." I lift her out of her crib and kiss her chubby little cheeks. "You have a soggy bottom. Let's change your diaper."

"No." She shakes her head just like her mother. It makes me laugh. "No."

"Yes," I say.

"*No.*"

"The one word you can say as clear as a bell."

I lay her on her changing table and make quick work of cleaning her up. She manages to chant her displeasure the entire time while trying to wiggle off the table and pull anything off me she can grab.

"Up!" she says, flexing her little fingers at me.

I pretend to bite one of them, making her giggle.

"Come on, you little monster," I say, picking her up. "Now remember, Uncle Ripley is bad. Can you say *bad*?"

Her eyes light up as we round the corner. "Dada!"

## The Situation

The name is a squeal as much as it is a word. I'm not sure I've ever seen Gannon smile so wide in his life—not even the time he punched Renn in the stomach and Mom didn't believe him.

*Ah, the good ole days.*

I hand Ivy off to her father and join Carys in the kitchen.

"I'm sorry if I upset you," I say. "I probably should've approached that differently. I'm a third party here, and this isn't about me."

"No, I get it. If someone hurt Gannon, I'd act the same way."

We watch him play with Ivy. The asshole who never said a nice thing to anyone is putty in a toddler's hands. It's almost hard to believe ... but also not.

I can't imagine what he feels when he looks at his little girl. I know what I feel like when I look at her, and she's not mine. But for Gannon—to see himself and the woman he loves in one little person who is delighted to see him every day? That must feel better than anything in the world.

"You love her, don't you?" Carys asks softly. "Aurora, not Ivy."

I nod.

"Does it scare you that it's happened so fast?" she asks.

I sigh, pulling my gaze to my best friend. "No, it doesn't scare me. I've always told you that I would know the woman for me when I met her."

"That you have."

"I think she's a little scared shitless. I'm trying to keep some distance so she can breathe, but—"

"But your style is to smother, I know." She chuckles. "Make sure you bring her to your birthday party."

"Hey, about that ... I have an idea. It's not fully formed, and I'm still getting it all together. But I might have a request."

"You can't make requests for your birthday party," Gannon says. "That's not how it works."

"And hold off on selling the Raptors," I say. "Let me talk to my girl."

Gannon's brows lift, and he gives me a smug smile.

"I'll call you," I tell Carys, walking backward to the door. I wave at their little family. "But, right now, I have to get to work—unlike some people who just stay home all day. I love you guys."

"Watch it!" Gannon says.

I laugh as I walk out the door.

## Chapter Twenty-Five

Aurora

"Hey," I say, answering the phone as soon as I see Tate's name light up the screen. "Can you hold on for one second?"

"Absolutely."

I drop the phone to my side. "Can you finish getting that together and bring it to my office, Tally? I need to take this call."

"That's better, anyway. You make me nervous when you stand over my shoulder."

"I do not."

She laughs as I leave her office.

The building is relatively empty, with most of the staff leaving around four o'clock. The usual chatter between coworkers, phones ringing, and computers dinging is quiet. You can almost hear yourself think.

"Sorry," I say, heading down the hall. "Tally and I have been fighting with the tech team all afternoon."

"If you have work to do, ignore me."

I slip inside my office and close the door behind me.

"You're very hard to ignore, Mr. Brewer. I've tried."

He chuckles.

"Also, you're my boss." I sit behind my desk. "I'm pretty much required to answer your calls."

"I'm going to start saving all of my questions until we're in the office."

I laugh. "That's unfair. I answer everything you ask me."

"True, but at work, you'll try harder to answer them the way I like them answered."

"Whatever."

"I'm on my way to the office. Should arrive in about twenty minutes. Do you need anything?"

My heart flutters at his thoughtfulness. He has so much to do, and so many people counting on him, yet he manages to see if I need anything on his way in. I didn't know there were real men like this out there.

I could have saved a lot of heartache if I had known.

"I need some things, but nothing you can give me here," I say, grinning.

He growls, making me laugh.

"I stopped by Gannon's this morning," he says.

*Oh.* "Did you?"

"I did. And I told them about us."

I sink into my chair as blood rushes to my face. I knew he'd do this eventually, but I didn't realize it would be so soon.

My emotions are all over the place when it comes to Carys. We did have a conversation, and yes, it ended well. But we said we'd meet for drinks, and we didn't. The blame is on me more than her because she told me she was pregnant, and I didn't reach out.

Maybe she hung up the phone that day and decided I was a

bitch. She could've boxed me up with her father in her brain and burned us both to the ground. Carys has always been a sweetheart, and I don't think she'd do that. But if she did, the news that I'm dating her best friend—her baby's uncle—probably wouldn't go over well.

A few years ago, I would have felt like I own the blame of not maintaining that relationship. That everything's always my fault. But I've grown since then. I've learned. Evolved. And I feel simply cautious and conscious that Carys might not be okay with me in her best friend's life.

"And how did that go?" I ask, wincing.

"Gannon high-fived me for banging the hot stepmommy."

"*He did not.*"

"You're right. He didn't." Tate laughs. "Gannon has never high-fived anyone in his life."

I exhale into the phone. *Bastard.*

"They were both perfectly fine with it," he says. "Why wouldn't they be?"

"I don't know."

"Carys said to make sure you come to my birthday party, and I assured her you'd be there."

I sit up. "*Your birthday?*"

"Yeah."

"It's soon?"

"It's the fourth, and we're having a surprise party for me at Jason's."

*What?* "How is it a surprise party if you know about it?"

"Because surprise parties are more fun. Bianca's coming with Foxx and Emery. Mom's going to make it, too, I think. It's going to be fun. You'll love it."

I swallow past the lump in my throat.

I'm not sure if I'm ready to meet *the whole family.*

*Wouldn't it be better to meet them in small groups? Next year, perhaps?*

"What did you have for lunch?" he asks.

My stomach growls at the mention of food. "Nothing. I couldn't get away from my desk."

"Unacceptable."

"Sorry to disappoint you, but I'm starving. Would you like to go to the movies tonight?"

"Sure. What do you want to see?"

"The concession stand."

He snorts. "What?"

"I just want a big bucket of popcorn with extra butter. We can eat and then sleep through the movie."

Tires squeal in the distance.

"Shit." An engine roars, and I hear a downshift. "If that's what you want to do, that's what we'll do."

"Are you okay?"

"Yeah. Traffic."

"I found your washer and dryer this morning and started a load with your sheets. I don't have a lot of hope that the blueberry stains will come out."

"I hope not."

My brows pinch together. "Why? We ruined a perfect set of sheets."

"I'd rather have the memories than perfection." His engine roars. "I have to make a quick stop, and then I'll be back in the office. I have something to discuss with you. Can you pencil me in for a quick chat?"

"It's going to cost you."

He laughs. "Talk soon."

"Bye."

I lay my phone on my desk and breathe a sigh of relief.

*"Gannon high-fived me for banging the hot stepmommy."*

I laugh, shaking my head. It's a goofy line, said to make me relax, and I appreciate Tate for knowing I needed the levity. I wonder, however, if he knows that all these references to various forms of parenting are making me think.

## The Situation

I'm not sure I'm ready for marriage again, but I am becoming more certain that I do want to have children. My age makes me worry. The fact that I'm not married and can't even see the marriage path clearly makes me worry even more. But the more I think about having a baby, the more certain I feel that I want to experience motherhood.

*The part that worries me the most?* I can't imagine sharing a child with anyone but Tate.

I trust him more than I've ever trusted a man. He's the greatest to me. His employees adore him. The way he talks about his family proves that there's not a bad bone in his body because if anyone else talks shit about another person, it's their sibling.

He's the kind of man with whom you'd want to raise a child.

Smart. Kind. A huge heart.

I look up as a knock sounds against my door.

"Come in," I say, clearing my throat.

Tally barges in and plops into a chair. "I still hate it."

"Oh no."

"You know how they say that there are people for radio and people for television?"

"Kind of."

"Well, there are people made to work in tech and people made to make it pretty. Those people are not the same." She slides a folder across my desk. "These are the quotes that Charlie requested for a multitude of marketing items. Tate said to give them to you."

"To me?"

I open the folder and flip through the pages. Each one is for an amount larger than the previous one. There are stacks of bills, all in alphabetical order, and the running total in my head makes me sweat.

This is crazy.

"This invoice is for fifty thousand dollars." I gasp. "I can't approve this."

"Why not?"

I look up and find Tate leaning against the doorframe.

"It's not my money to spend," I tell him.

"What do you think when you look at those invoices?" he asks.

I leaf through a few on top. "Honestly? I love Charlie, and he does an amazing job. But I have no idea why we're paying these prices. We can get a lot of this done much, much cheaper."

Tally stands. "I'm going to go fight the tech department. Remember, I leave early tomorrow. Gotta get my pickleball physical."

"What?" Tate asks, amused.

"It's a long story, Mr. Brewer. Just know that I'm a pickleball wizard. I can't be stopped."

"Good to know," he says, laughing as she struts out of my office with her ponytail swishing behind her.

He comes in and sets a bucket of theater popcorn on my desk.

"Holy crap," I say, laughing in disbelief. "Where did you get that?"

"The cinema down the street."

"You just walked in and got it?"

He shrugs as he sits in the chair Tally just occupied. "Yeah. You can do that."

"Are you sure?"

"I just did it. I'm sure."

My heart swells, and I can't stop grinning. "Thank you. This is the sweetest thing."

"So why is your intern going to fight the tech department?" Tate asks, taking a handful of popcorn.

"We're having some issues with the guys not listening to the adjustments we request. I'm going down there to have a face-to-face with them tomorrow."

Tate arches a brow.

"The website is the home of the organization," I say. "It can't look like shit. And if they can't understand what we're going for, I'll find someone who can."

He grins. "I like you fiery."

## The Situation

"You should've seen me an hour ago. I threatened a printer. Had it quaking in its boots."

His chest shakes as he laughs.

"What did you want to talk to me about?" I ask, tossing a couple of perfectly popped kernels in my mouth. "By the way, you buttered this like a popcorn pro."

"Good to know. I'll add that to my résumé." He takes another handful from the bucket. "So I wanted to talk to you about a hypothetical situation."

"Gotta love those."

He reaches behind him and shuts the door.

"This stays between us," he says.

"Of course."

"If you were given a clean slate—that is, starting from scratch—what would you do differently to make this franchise a success?"

"*Anything?*" I ask.

"Anything."

This is a marketing lover's dream.

"Safe space?" I ask.

"Safe space."

"Okay, then." I rub my hands together. "First, I'd get rid of that terrible Raptors mascot and replace it with something elevated yet relatable. We'd build an iconic logo that's fresh and marketable—something that looks great on merch. That sounds crazy, but it isn't. Great merch is easy marketing, and the best brands have it figured out."

"Those are great points."

"I'm not done." I chuckle, just getting started. "New colors that don't scream Midwestern US high school basketball."

"That's an interesting comparison."

I shrug. "That's exactly what the dusty black and crimson screams, and that's not the message we want to put out."

"No, it's not."

"With that said, we'd update the facilities and overhaul the arena.

Give people a reason to want to come and spend their money here. Make it a good time."

He smiles, grabbing another few kernels.

"I don't know a lot about hockey," I admit. "But I'd look at the coaching staff and roster. We need people who are a draw. People love winners, sure, but they also love people with a story. People they can root for or against. It doesn't matter."

"I love that."

"Stronger digital platforms. Involve the fans and increase engagement. Start traditions. People love a tradition!"

"Okay," he says, amused. "That's enough. I can see the picture you're painting, and I love it."

I grin. "You didn't even take notes."

"I didn't have to. I happen to have infinite access to the notebook."

"Oh, you do, do you?"

"I hope so."

Our gazes connect, and I've never felt more listened to. I've also never felt so comfortable letting someone see inside me.

*I hope so, too.*

It's terrifying even to let that thought run through my mind because things have been great—but there's still time for things to go to shit.

And they do often go to shit.

"Don't," he says, throwing a piece of popcorn at me.

I try to catch it in my mouth, but miss. "Don't what?"

"Get out of your head."

"I'm not in my head," I lie.

"You're questioning everything. It's like you have a button in your head that turns on when things go too smoothly." He leans forward. "Stop expecting things to crumble. Expect them to go right."

I frown. "But things do crumble."

"Not when they're built right." He stands and plants a kiss on the

## The Situation

top of my head. "I gotta go take care of a few things at the Brewer Group offices. I might be a few hours."

I nod. "Call me later."

"Of course. See ya, gorgeous."

"Bye."

With a simple smile that I feel in the depths of my heart, he walks out.

But he does leave the popcorn.

# Chapter Twenty-Six

## Tate

I grip the steering wheel and hit the ramp toward home.

The dark sky is filled with millions of silver stars. The air is a perfect seventy degrees. I feel lighter, happier than I've felt in a long damn time.

I can't wipe the smile off my face.

*How did I get so lucky to find a woman who's as brilliant as she is beautiful?*

Gannon's announcement has rolled around in my head nonstop. At first, I was certain I'd just cash out and go home. But the more I thought about it, the more I realized an opportunity was in front of me, and I'd be remiss to discount it altogether.

Hockey isn't my thing, but business is my jam. I also happen to love the idea of wiping everything Reid fucking Brewer created and starting something new—something I built, something I could make successful if for no other reason than spite.

He never thought I'd make anything out of myself. Out of all the kids, maybe besides Renn, he disliked me the most. So an opportunity to do something he couldn't do in a world he created? It's at least worth a consideration ... and that's without considering Aurora.

I wasn't sure what her response would be when I asked her how she would recreate the hockey team if given a clean slate. I wanted to gauge her interest without putting her on the spot—really feel out the possibility of working together on something of this magnitude.

If it works, how special would that be?

*"First, I'd get rid of that terrible Raptors mascot and replace it with something elevated yet relatable. We'd build an iconic logo that's fresh and marketable—something that looks great on merch. That sounds crazy, but it isn't. Great merch is easy marketing, and the best brands have it figured out."*

She's right. Spot-fucking-on.

"New colors that don't scream Midwestern US high school basketball."

I laugh. She's not wrong, though.

"With that said, we'd update the facilities and overhaul the arena. Give people a reason to want to come and spend their money here. Make it a good time.

"We need people who are a draw. People love winners, sure, but they also love people with a story. People they can root for or against. It doesn't matter.

"Stronger digital platforms. Involve the fans and increase engagement. Start traditions. People love a tradition!"

Every word out of her mouth is inspiring, thought-provoking, and invigorating.

My girl is a superstar. I can't wait to watch her take hold of this project and mold it into something we're both proud of ... because it would be ours.

"Might as well start building shit together now because I have no plans to ever let her go."

*I've fallen in love with her, and I fucking hope the feeling is mutual.*

# Chapter Twenty-Seven

## Aurora

"What are we doing? Tate asks, stretching out beside me on his bed.

"Rotting."

"*Rotting*." He tests the words on his tongue. "What the hell does *rotting* mean?"

"It means we rot."

He makes a face. "Which means what?"

"It means we're going to lie here and do nothing. No effort. We'll get up to go to the bathroom and refill drinks. That's it. Think of it as if you're charging your batteries."

He grabs his cock and shakes it. "My batteries don't charge unless I'm plugged in."

I laugh as I curl up next to him.

We've spent every day together for the past couple of weeks, and every day it feels a little more like we've been doing it forever. We have our routine—Tate gets up an hour before I do and wakes me before he leaves. I usually get back to the house before him, so I start dinner, and he comes home at the end and helps me finish the recipe.

For someone who hasn't lived with anyone before, at least as far as I know, Tate has adjusted very quickly. Surprisingly, he's easy to live with, too. *Not that I've moved in—that would be way too fast.*

His circle has also been kind to me. We had dinner with Renn and Blakely one night, and his brother Ripley swung by to borrow something. He was a slightly different version of Tate, and we got along great.

So apart from Tate's not-so-subtle suggestions about getting married, it's been pretty perfect.

Work, on the other hand, is a different story. I'm not sure what the hell is going on there. Energetically working toward new goals and a new direction has just ... stopped. Tally and I have very little on our plates. If anyone knows what's happening, nobody's saying a word.

Not even Tate.

*Shouldn't he still be leading us and overseeing the department's functions?* It's so ... weird. And I don't know what to make of it.

"What do you think about taking a vacation next week?" he asks. "Let's get through the weekend, then spend a few days away—just the two of us."

My chest constricts as I read between the lines.

I've been dancing around this for the past few days, too. Tate has been finagling a way to get me alone. He's tried to take me back to Columbus for *nostalgic purposes*. I mentioned wanting to see Costa Rica, and he offered to sort that for me immediately. He even booked a house in Sedona, Arizona, but I made him get a refund.

I know what he's trying to do, and I'm trying to avoid it like the plague.

"How do you think we have time to get away for a trip like that?" I ask. "Charlie just tendered his official resignation this week after his mom's passing. We've had to mothball the rebrand for reasons I still don't understand, and I feel like all the work that Tally and I have put in over the past couple of months has been for nothing, and nobody cares."

"I care."

"Do you, though?"

"Of course," he says, stroking my back. "I care about everything that affects you."

"Then why won't you tell me what's going on?"

"Because I'm under an NDA at the moment. I'll explain it all as soon as I can." He bends down and kisses my forehead. "It'll be worth it. Just hold on for a bit longer."

I sigh, shoving away from him and sitting up.

"My mom called today," he says. "She's flying in tomorrow for my party and can't wait to meet you."

"I'm excited to meet her. Your sister's family will be there, too, right?"

He nods, clearing his throat.

If this week hadn't been so heavy at work, I might be looking forward to meeting Tate's entire family tomorrow. Because, in theory, it's a beautiful gesture. In reality, though, it's terrifying.

*What if they don't like me? What if Carys is cold and unfriendly?* I couldn't blame her. *What if his mother thinks I'm too old for her baby boy?* That wouldn't be a blamable offense, either.

And God knows what Tate's told them. He seems to be telling the world that I'm Mrs. Tate Brewer. And every time that happens, every time he casts a joke out into our little bubble about our "marriage," I react viscerally.

I know I've worked hard to get through the trauma of my last marriage, and I know I'm a stronger woman now, but the idea of leaping from one marriage into another so quickly freaks me out.

It's not him that's the problem. He's as close to perfection as you can get.

I'm afraid to say this directly because I might lose him. He might finally believe I'm not worth the trouble.

But not saying anything doesn't lend itself to healthy communication, which can then lead to an unhealthy relationship. So I'm royally screwed either way I go.

"Can I talk to you about something?" I ask.

"Sure."

I sigh, not wanting to discuss this, but not seeing a way out, either.

"I had two people come up to me today and congratulate me on my engagement," I say. "Because we are getting married, apparently."

He smirks. "You better not be marrying anyone else."

"That's not the point."

"What is it then?"

I hang my head. This is going to be just as tricky as I feared.

"First, we aren't engaged," I say. "So it makes it super awkward for me to try to backtrack and explain that I don't know where they heard that, but it's false."

"Would it be easier just to get engaged?"

"No."

He pretends to focus on the muted television across the room. I nearly laugh because his pout is the biggest I've ever seen. But I hold strong and manage not to crack. This sweet, precious man has put marriage on a pedestal, and I truly hate that I'm the one attempting to remove it from its perch. *Because when marriage falls, it can shatter. And those sharp pieces cut you to the core.*

"What would be easier is if you stopped telling people that," I say. "Then I wouldn't have to defend myself."

"I didn't realize that someone wanting to be with you was offensive."

I groan. "Please don't pick a fight with me."

"I'm not," he says. "But I feel like we're just treading water pointlessly when we could be doing so many huge, fun things."

"Maybe I'm fine with treading water for a bit. It'll make my muscles stronger to carry the big things later."

"You don't need to be strong. I'll carry everything for you."

## The Situation

I run my hand down his arm, feeling the ripples of his muscles under my palm.

I've avoided having a frank version of this conversation for days. But each day, I feel more pressure to fold—to acquiesce to what Tate wants me to do. Namely, make him my whole personality.

That's what it feels like, anyway.

Spending time with Tate Brewer is one of the most surreal experiences of my life. I wouldn't trade it or him for anything or anyone. And I hope to spend the rest of my life at his side.

I've fallen hard for him. *I've fallen in love with him.* And I never thought I'd be on this side of love again. Not in the foreseeable future, anyway.

But he's so charismatic, so capable, so overwhelming that it makes it almost impossible to keep my head above water.

I need a minute to breathe without the air scented with his cologne. And I need him to be okay with that. *I need him to hear what I need right now.*

Because to date, he's been extremely good at that.

*Please hear me, Tate. Please know this will be better for us.*

"Since the Raptors are still on hold and I just sit in the office with nothing to do, I was thinking about taking a couple of days off next week," I say.

"Sure. What do you want to do?"

I shrug. "I was thinking about spending time with Jamie. She mentioned that she's struggling, and if I'm not going to be doing any work with the Raptors, I'd rather be doing something productive, if that makes sense."

He nods, but I'm not sure it makes sense to him. *Oh, the comprehension of a billionaire who doesn't need to work.*

"I'd still be in town if the Raptors stuff starts up again," I say.

"For sure." He pulls me in for a hug. "Whatever makes you happy, gorgeous."

I smile against him.

"You know I don't mean anything harmful when I tell people

you're going to be my wife, right?" he asks. "I just feel like I've hit the jackpot."

"I feel that way, too." I press a kiss to his shoulder and sit upright.

"Really?"

"Yeah, but if I'm being honest, it's starting to overwhelm me a little bit."

He flinches. "It is?"

"Yeah."

"Why?"

"Because I'm feeling pressured," I say.

"Are you saying you don't want me talking about us to anyone?"

There's a pain buried in his blues that breaks my heart.

"That's not what I'm saying at all," I say. "Look, Tate, I've been candid with you about not being sure about marriage. It doesn't mean I don't want to be with you—"

"You don't want to marry me?"

I sigh. "I didn't say that."

"Yeah, you sort of did."

I sit crisscross applesauce, facing him, trying to remain calm and in control.

"I said that I'm not sure about marriage. In general," I say. "Not specifically to you."

He scoots up until his back is against the headboard. "I thought we were past this."

"No, *you* got past it because you ignored me."

"What are you saying?" he asks, his jaw tensing.

I take his hand in mine. "I'm saying that I've been very clear about being unsure about marriage or, if I decide to do it, when that'll happen."

"All I want is you," he says, brushing my hair out of my face.

"All I want is you, too. But you must understand that I don't want to do it on your timeline."

He drops his hands and shakes his head. "I don't understand it. I don't understand why it's so hard for you to want to be mine."

## The Situation

"I am yours. Can't I be yours without a ring on my finger?"

"Can't you just wear a ring and be done with it?"

I take a long, deep breath in and blow it out before I lose my cool.

"Marriage to you seems simple." *We haven't even said I love you.* "I know you said your parents didn't have a good marriage, but you still seem to have it on a pedestal."

He studies me, but I have no idea if what I'm saying is landing or not.

I scooch closer. "Marriage can be hard. We've only spent five minutes together, and we haven't …" I pause. I'm not going to mention love in this space. Not when I'm angry and he's not hearing me. "I think we need more time together before we discuss getting married," I say. "Because when I think of marriage, it's tainted with the feelings of losing my independence, of giving up control. Being told what to do and not having an equal voice in things."

*And I can't do that again. I won't.*

He narrows his eyes.

"I'm not eager to do that again, Tate."

"So you don't trust me?"

"This has nothing to do with you."

"Oh, okay," he says, nodding like he's pissed. "So I waited my whole life for the one girl who I want to spend my life with, and then I get told to hang on. She might want to be with you. She might not. She might have your children. She might not."

"Why can't I just have you?" I ask, holding my arms out to the sides. "Why do I have to come with a piece of paper that a judge stamps?"

"Why can't *I* just have *you*?" he asks.

"You can! Just not at warp speed!"

He looks at me like I'm out of my mind.

I don't know if I'm tired from the week, or if I'm stressed by being hounded by this question every day. I might just be pissed that I'm dealing with feeling out of control yet again.

"I'm not saying I won't ever want to marry you, or that I don't want to have your children, because I actually fucking do," I say, my voice rising. "But I want to do it on my time. I'm sick and tired of having to make my life's decisions on someone else's clock. If I marry you someday, I don't want to have any lingering trauma in the back of my mind that I carry into our union. I need to heal, Tate."

His face falls.

"I told you this from the beginning," I say. "I told you I wanted a one-night stand so this didn't happen. I didn't leave you my name or number—why? *So this didn't happen.*"

"Well, it happened."

"What about you telling me you'd be patient? Are you tired of waiting?" A swell of emotion lurches up my throat. I swallow it back as best as I can, but my voice is hoarse. "Did you finally decide that I'm more trouble than I'm worth?"

He doesn't move as I climb off the bed because I won't let him see me cry.

I'll never let a man see me cry again.

I make quick work of getting dressed and am jogging down the steps when Tate comes out of his room.

"Aurora," he says, from the landing.

I pause, stopping and looking up at him.

The pain in his eyes is the same I feel ripping through me. There's no point in making it worse.

I tuck my chin, bolt to my car, and go home.

## Chapter Twenty-Eight

Aurora

"Honey, I'm home!" I say as I enter the salon.

I thought it would be a funny way to announce myself, but it just stings my heart. *Too soon.*

"Out front," Jamie yells. "Bring a can of disinfectant with you, please!"

"Sounds like I'm walking into something." I rummage around in the storage closet. "Where are you keeping the cleaning stuff now? Wait! Found it!"

I snag the can and carry it with me to the front of the building.

"Here," Jamie says, wiggling her fingers without looking at me. "Gimme."

"What are we disinfecting?" I ask, peering down at the floor, and see ... nothing. "What are you looking at?"

"Something moved right there. By the bottom of the chair."

I look again, but all I see is tile. "There's nothing there, Jamie."

She holds the can like a weapon—arm extended, eye lined up with the bottom of the barrel—and fires away.

I cough, fanning my face, and step back. "Okay! I think you got it."

She stops and peers down again. Unsatisfied, she blasts it for another five seconds for good measure.

"You told me you've been lonely, but you haven't said anything about seeing things," I say, hopping up in my old chair. "That might be a symptom of something."

"I'm not seeing things. It moved. I swear."

"Sure."

She rolls her eyes but comes to me with wide arms. "I missed you so damn much."

Her embrace is wide and warm. While it doesn't do the same things for me that Tate's hugs do, it's appreciated, nonetheless.

"The place looks good," I say, spinning in a half circle to observe my old haunts. "New lights in the windows? Nice."

"And a new basket for magazines. Oh! I finally replaced the cute little hand soap dispenser in the bathroom."

"It's about time."

"Right?" She sits in her chair and sighs. "You look good."

I half smile. "Yeah, well, thanks for lying to me."

"What's wrong?"

"Is it that obvious?"

"Honey, I've known you in various stages of life. I can tell when something is wrong. Spill it."

Tate's words ravage my mind again.

"*So I waited my whole life for the one girl who I want to spend my life with, and then I get told to hang on. She might want to be with you. She might not. She might have your children. She might not.*"

He didn't tell me he loved me. *Does he not love me? Does he think this is all too hard now?*

I consider telling her about my fight with Tate, but it feels too

## The Situation

heavy. My body hasn't processed it yet. And if my hormones haven't adjusted to meet my needs, I can't even start talking about it.

"Can we start with you?" I ask.

"Sure. You know I love to talk about myself."

I smile. "What's been happening around here? Catch me up with all the drama."

"You must really not want to talk if you're asking for drama. You always hate when the gossip starts."

I shrug. She's not wrong.

"Maddie was in yesterday," Jamie says. "New boyfriend, but it's not a new boyfriend. It's the one who left her at the bar downtown on Labor Day weekend."

"Oh yeah. I remember him. We had a name for him. What was it?"

"Dill Boy?" Jamie asks, shaking her head.

"No! Gherkins Boy! She said his penis looked like a sweet gherkin."

"Ha!" Jamie laughs. "I'll have to remind her about that."

"What about Onessa? I've been wondering about her cats."

Jamie nods knowingly. "Tigerlily has passed."

"Aw!"

"I know, I know. There was a funeral. I couldn't make it. Beebop seems to still be grieving. Onessa might get a new cat, but not another orange one. She's not sure."

"She should," I say, nodding.

"That's what I told her. Oh, and Phil was in. Remember him? He brought tuna salad in a margarine container and ate it while he waited."

My stomach recoils at the memory. We couldn't get that smell out of here for a week.

"You know how we thought Phil had a thing for Barbara?"

"Yeah ..."

"We were *so right*. That's unproven right now, but I heard it from an excellent source."

I laugh, the brick on my chest lifting just a bit.

Jamie watches me, trying to decide whether it's safe to test the waters on my drama. I still don't want to talk about it, but she is my best friend, and I could use an honest opinion.

I sigh. "Tate and I got into our first fight. Well, I don't know if it was a fight or not. We had a robust disagreement. How's that?"

"What about?"

"He wants things to get super serious, super fast."

"How do you feel about that?"

I get to my feet and slowly pace the salon. So many nights I've walked these floors trying to work something out. A marriage. A divorce. Rumors and financial issues. Bruises and heartbreak. The list goes on and on.

If the walls could talk in this place, the stories they could tell.

"I feel awful," I say, my heart squeezing at the look in his eyes when I left. "He's a great guy and means nothing but the best. I wouldn't have to pick between the bear or the man because Tate would slaughter them both for me."

"Great answer. Wrong question."

"Huh?"

"I asked you how you felt about him wanting to get serious, and you answered that you felt bad and he was a great guy. That wasn't what I asked you."

*Oh.* I take a deep breath. "I haven't told him this, but I love him."

Jamie flinches.

"I know. That's wild coming out of this mouth," I say, laughing sadly. "But I do. There's nothing not to love about him. It's crazy when I think about it because every time someone has told me they've fallen in love this fast, I've laughed at them. And now, here I am, knowing what love feels like for the first time and doing it in record time."

"Another great answer to the wrong question."

I spin around to face her. "What do you want me to say?"

"How. Do. You. Feel. About. Him. Wanting. To. Get. Serious?"

## The Situation

"You don't have to be a dick."

She points at me. "You're emotional, so I'm going to let that slide."

"Sorry," I say, heaving a breath. "I feel ..."

*How do I feel?*

I pace again, this time faster. I make a figure eight around two pillars on either side of the building.

"Talk it out," she says. "That's why you're here. You could've thought quietly in your car."

I look at her and shake my head.

"What? I'm not a trained counselor. You want my services? We're doing things my way."

"Okay," I say, resolved to get to the bottom of this. "I feel fine about getting serious with him. I see myself with him for the rest of my life. I want his babies. I want his stories after work. I'll even take his dirty laundry."

Especially blueberry sheets.

Tears well up in the corners of my eyes as I remember that night in his bed.

"But I don't want to get married. Not yet," I say. "Maybe not ever. And he wants it right now, and I can't give it to him. I feel ... *cursed*." I nearly spit the word out. "I don't want to curse us, you know?"

"Did you tell him this?"

"I tried to. We both got a little hotheaded, and that never bodes well for communication."

"No, it does not."

"I don't know what to do, Jamie."

She sits back in her chair. "I might not have a degree in counseling, but I do have a cosmetology degree, and it's basically the same thing—only I can do hair and nails."

I laugh. *God, that's so true.*

"Let's break this down," she says. "He wants to marry you. He doesn't want to date, right? He wants marriage."

"He wants me to be his wife."

She considers this. "That's really sweet, actually. But I know where you're coming from, and your concerns are valid. I'm going to deduce from this that buried down deep inside that Adonis body—which I know he has because I checked him out on Social—he's afraid of losing you. He wants you, or maybe the white picket fence thing, so much that each piece of the puzzle feels like he's building a foundation. So, without marriage, he can't get the whole picture."

"But things do crumble."

"Not when they're built right."

Silence fills my body as things start to make sense.

"Holy shit, Jamie. You might be right."

"Funny that you doubt me at all," she says, making a face. "Now, the other part of this is probably the fact that he's a billionaire stud who has never been told *no* a day in his life."

I snort.

"So your boy doesn't know how to compromise. He's acting like a brat. You did the right thing putting your foot down."

I hum, lifting my chin.

"But," she says, pointing a perfectly manicured nail my way, "you have to compromise, too. If you want this to work, that is."

"How? Marriage is my triggering event. I. Don't. Want. To. Get. Married."

"But you are fine with committing to him?"

I nod.

"Then figure out a way to do that."

"I can't. I can't give him what he wants."

"Bet you can." She winks. "You might have to think a minute, but you'll find a solution."

She gets up and heads into the back, leaving me alone.

*How does she think I can give him what he wants if it's something I can't do?* I groan. *I can't compromise on that. I can't half marry him. There's no other way of committing to him ...*

I stop pacing. My heartbeat quickens.

*Oh my God. There is a way.*

## The Situation

My palms sweat as I think things over. It's a crazy idea.
*But is it?*

The longer I contemplate it, the more it makes sense. The more I like it. The more I really want to make it happen.

I put a hand on my stomach and exhale.

"Did you figure it out yet?" Jamie asks.

I look at her over my shoulder as she enters the room. She stops in the doorway and takes me in, then nods.

"Yeah. You figured it out." She grins.

"He has a birthday party tomorrow," I say. "Maybe I write him a little note and give it to him there?"

"You don't want to go back over there tonight?"

I shake my head. As much as I do want to, I shouldn't. We need some time apart—if for no other reason than to ensure we know what we want.

"You don't happen to have some pretty stationery, do you?" I ask.

"Actually, yes. A customer left some out here a few weeks ago and never came back to get it. It's in the top desk drawer."

I nearly jog to her office and yank open the drawer. There lies a cream-colored notepad with faint white and gray swirls in the background. It reminds me of his countertops.

I sit down and pull the pad out, along with the pen that goes with it. Then I stare at the paper and try to figure out how to say what's on my mind.

After a deep breath, I start writing ...

# Chapter Twenty-Nine

## Tate

"What are you doing in here?" Mimi asks, groaning as she settles into her recliner. A party hat is perched on top of her head, and a string secures it around her chin. She's adorably ridiculous.

I'm stretched out on her sofa, listening to the partygoers celebrating my birthday as they laugh outside by the pool.

"Thought about taking a nap," I say.

I tilt my head, so I look behind me and catch her giving me the strangest look.

"I could use a nap," she says. "Want to get in bed with me?"

My chest shakes as I laugh even though I don't feel like it.

Last night was the first time I've seen Aurora mad. It was also the first time that I felt like a fucking asshole and regretted it. I've never not known how to fix a problem with a woman until she stormed out of my house … and refused my calls.

## The Situation

I cover my face with my hands and groan.

"Either tell me what's wrong or get out of my house," Mimi says, her tone teasing.

"I fucked up."

"I gathered that. How?"

My hands slide down my face, pulling my lip as they go. "I showed my ass."

"Nobody's going to be mad at that."

"You're not helping, Mimi."

"I'm old. If you don't get to the point fast, I might croak."

I sit up, sick of myself.

"Here, I'll help," she says. "You messed up with Girlfriend #2. Take it from there."

Despite my shitty mood, I can't help but smile at Girlfriend #1.

"I had this image of what my life was going to be like now that I met her," I say, realizing just how much of a jerk I sound like when I say it aloud. "She disagreed. I pushed. And last night, she walked out on me."

Mimi whistles through her dentures.

"*Yeah.*" I nod as I exhale. "Like I said, I fucked up."

"Well, you don't lie. That's a plus."

I glance at her out of the corner of my eye. She's grinning.

"First of all, what hill was this you were willing to die on?" she asks.

"Marriage."

"Oh, Tate." She sighs as if this might kill her. "You're proof God can't give brains and beauty to the same person."

*He did to Aurora, but I don't want to argue that point now.*

"I just want to marry her," I say. "I love the fucking shit out of her, Mimi. I want to take care of her and spoil her rotten. I want to have a family with her. What's wrong with that?"

She groans. "Let me see how many crayons I have lying here so I can draw you a picture."

"You're so funny."

"Look, she put you in your place. She looked into those beautiful eyes and wasn't dazzled. And good for her."

"Whose side are you on?"

"This time? Not yours."

I stare at her. *Traitor.*

"It's time you learned the art of compromise," she says. "That's where you take a little. They take a little. You give some, and they give some."

"I know what it is."

"Then why didn't you do it?"

My thoughts drift back through my conversation with Aurora. *Why didn't I compromise?*

I bury my head in my hands as my words ring through my brain.

*"So I waited my whole life for the one girl who I want to spend my life with, and then I get told to hang on. She might want to be with you. She might not. She might have your children. She might not."*

There were alternate ways of fixing this besides demanding that I get my way. *Why would she even want to marry me if I'm going to be such a dick about it?*

"Have you talked to her since she left?" Mimi asks.

I shake my head.

"You should've had your ass over there and been on your knees before she got home," she says. "Didn't we just have a conversation about this—about showing her what you mean?"

"You're really mean today."

"Somebody has to be. Someone must remind you that you can't be a brat."

My face pops up to face hers, my eyes wide. "A brat?"

"A brat." She crosses her frail little arms over her chest. "You can't always get what you want."

"I know that, okay? Chill out."

"No one says that anymore."

"How do you ... Never mind." I sigh, my face turning red. "I got scared. That's the truth of it. I felt rejected. I panicked. I've been making all of these plans and all I could see was my whole life falling down—because it started with her. And I hurt her in the process." I hang my head. "Fuck."

"Now we're getting somewhere."

"I gotta fix this."

"Well, right now, there's a party going on out there, and a bunch of people traveled a long way to see you. Spend some time with them and then stop pussyfooting around and go get your girl."

I wipe my hands down my jeans. "Thanks, Mimi. I love you."

"Aw, Tate. I love you, too. But this round of your bullshit about killed me. You owe me one shirtless trip around the neighborhood next week."

Laughing, I press a kiss to her cheek. "You got it."

"Close that door behind you. I'm going to take a little nap."

"Okay."

I let myself out of Mimi's cottage and step into the warm sunlight. My eyes scan the crowd, looking for Aurora in the off chance she shows up. But I don't see her.

I really don't expect to.

"There's my boy," Mom says, pulling me into a hug. "Happy birthday, sweetheart."

"Thanks, Mama. I'm glad you came, even if it's really to see the babies."

She laughs like I'm kidding.

"You look good," I say. "You look happy."

"I am." She beams. "I really, truly am. And it's nice to be back home. I miss Nashville."

There's a twist in her eye that pulls on my heart. She has too many memories here—both bad and good. She had to give up so much because of Dad.

"Lookie there, Ives." Ripley stops alongside us, holding Ivy.

"Hey, watch this," I say, letting Ivy grab my finger. "Ivy, say Tate!"

"Ta!"

"Oh, my goodness," Mom says, giggling. "That's so precious."

I look at Ripley and wink.

His smirk grows deeper than mine. "Watch this." He bounces Ivy around until she's facing him. "Ivy, say Rip!"

"Rrrrrrrrrrrrrrrrrrrip!"

"Sucka," Ripley says, walking away with the baby and a victory. *On my birthday.*

"Hey, Tate!" Jason's wife Chloe yells from the back porch. "Gannon wants to see you in the house."

*Oh, great. This day keeps getting better.*

---

Aurora

Voices and music drift from the back of the massive home with the long driveway. Cars worth more than most people's gross income line both sides of the street. I'd second-guess this is my destination except there's a sign on the front lawn that says *Happy birthday, Tate!*

I'm not sure I should be here. Actually, I'm pretty sure I should go. But this is Tate's birthday, a day he loves, and I want to wish him a great year.

And hopefully not goodbye.

I should've taken his calls last night. But every time the phone rang, my stomach would knot, and I'd convince myself we needed a little breathing room to think. In reality, I was just too nervous to come up with the right words to say.

"Aurora?"

*The Situation*

I turn to my left and see Carys standing on the porch. She immediately comes down the stairs and crosses the lawn.

"Hi," I say, my smile wobbly.

Before I can say anything else, she pulls me in a big hug.

"It's so good to see you," she says. "I'm glad you came."

"I wasn't sure if I should."

Her eyes are crystal clear and full of joy. I'm happy for her.

"How have you been?" I ask. "How is your baby?"

"Ivy is her name, and she's wonderful. Growing so fast. How about you?"

I laugh nervously. "I'm good. Been busy."

"Tate keeps you hoppin'. There's no doubt about that."

My smile falters, and Carys doesn't miss it.

She stands with me beneath the warm sun, feeling the wind dance across our skin. Neither of us speaks for the longest time. We just exist in the same space, and it's all I could ask for from her.

"This family is loud," she says softly. "They're tactile—definite huggers."

I grin. "They're a little overwhelming."

"Oh, girl, I know. But it's worth it. Trust me. They will fight for you," she says. "They will move mountains for you. Because if you're Gannon's, or Renn's, or Chloe's, *or Tate's*—you belong to us all."

Tears fill my eyes as she looks at me.

What a sweet, wonderful girl. Her father didn't deserve her, and I'm so glad she's found a safe, soft spot to land.

"I don't know what's going on," she says. "But I did see Tate a bit ago, and he looks like a wounded puppy."

I chuckle, wiping my eyes.

"Be tough with him," she says. "But be ready to forgive him too. Because, unlike other men that we know, this guy is one of the best. I know. I have a slightly older version of him."

I smile, pulling her into another hug.

"Thank you," I say.

"Of course. Now let's really meet for drinks this time."

I laugh, and it feels so good. "Yes. Let's do that."

"Come on. I'll show you to the party."

My breaths are strangled as my nerves get the best of me. A part of me wants to hand Carys the card and run like my life depends on it. I'm already emotional. *What if I see Tate and we cause a scene?*

I can't do that to him.

*Fuck. I shouldn't be here.*

"Hey, Carys," I say, stopping in my tracks.

"Yeah?"

I hand her the card with Tate's name on the front. "Can you give this to him for me? I just, um ... I need to go."

"Sure. We'd love for you to stay."

I shake my head as the tears start to well again. "Thank you. I'll call you for drinks next week."

Before I turn into a blubbering mess, I turn and walk down the street toward my car.

---

Tate

"Tate!" Carys runs to me like a dog is chasing her. "I have been looking everywhere for you."

"And I've been standing here talking to Bianca."

"Hi, Bianca," Carys says, then immediately turns her attention to me. She slams an envelope in my hand and then shoves me toward the side of the house. "Go."

*I'm so confused.* "Where?"

She stands in front of me, panting. "Aurora is here."

"What?"

"She was here. I saw her out front. She panicked, asked me to give you this, and is headed to her car. Go!"

I take off running to the front of the house.

"Go left on the road!" she shouts.

I sprint down the driveway, my heart pounding. Perspiration gathers between my shoulder blades as I trek onto the road. I look to my right, then to my left.

"*Where are you?*" I ask, scanning every driveway until I spot the last car in the line. And, just in front of it, is my girl.

"Aurora!" I shout, my jog turning into a sprint. "Wait!"

She jumps, looking over her shoulder. Her eyes find mine.

Even from this distance, and in this situation, I can see her love for me. I can see the pain inflicted on her. I can see the rest of my life.

Somehow, someway.

"Hey." I pant, stopping a few feet from her. "Carys said you were here."

She's beautiful in a pale blue dress that shows off her delicate shoulders. Her hair is piled on top of her head. There are bags beneath her eyes.

I want to touch her—to reach out and pull her close. But I don't deserve that. I broke our trust.

"I'm sorry," I say, holding her gaze. "I tried to call and apologize. Then, when you didn't answer, I figured coming by your house wouldn't be a good idea."

She almost grins.

"I was wrong. Selfish. Childish. Mimi called me a brat."

She bites her lip to keep from smiling.

"I have no right to tell you what to do, or to pressure you into doing anything," I say. "No matter my intentions, it was wrong. And I will never do anything like that again."

"Mimi called you a brat?"

"She did. And she was right." I shrug. "I want you in whatever way you'll consider letting me have you. I should've been more considerate of you, and I wasn't, and I hate myself for it."

"So what are you proposing?"

"Whatever you want. You call the shots. You're in control."

Her eyes soften.

"I want you to know that marriage is always on the table. Fifty years from now, it'll still be there. But I won't bring it up again," I say. "I'm not going to hurt you by making you think about terrible things. How stupid was I?"

"So no marriage?" she asks.

"I love you, Aurora Johnson. I'd rather have you in my life and arms and not be married, than not have you at all."

She nods, her breaths coming in deeper. "Did you read your card?"

"What card?" I look down at my hand. "Oh, no. Carys shoved it at me, then hurled me toward the road."

She fights a giggle. "Open it."

The top of the envelope is tucked into the back. I free it and pull the card out of the sleeve. Aurora watches me nervously as I open the card.

Her handwriting fills up most of the blank space.

## The Situation

*Happy birthday, Tate.*

*You're impossible to shop for because you have everything a man could want. Well, except for two things.*

*First, I love you. I might have some hang-ups regarding pieces of paper proving a relationship, but I give you my heart. It's yours.*

*Second, I know you want a family, and I do, too. And there's no other man in the world that I trust to be my child's father.*

*This setup is a little unconventional, but the idea of starting a family with you fills me with happiness. If I don't have kids with you, I likely won't have any. And I really want to be a mother.*

*The choices are yours.*

*Love,*

*Aurora*

"Are you fucking serious?" I drop the note to my side and look at Aurora in disbelief. "You're serious?"

She stands in front of me, our chests nearly touching. She peers up at me through her thick lashes.

"You don't think having a baby together is going too fast?" I ask.

She laughs. "I'm forty, okay? I don't have much longer left."

"Forty?" I make a face, and she slaps me on the chest. "Damn, girl. We better skip the party and get busy."

"Keep it up and I'll rescind my proposal."

"It's written down. It's pretty much a contract at this point."

She lifts up and tries to kiss me. Instead, I pick her up and wrap her legs around my waist.

"I love you," I say, pressing soft kisses on her lips. "I missed you so much last night."

She hums as I continue to kiss her.

"We have a lot to talk about, huh?" I ask, brushing strands of hair off her face.

"There's no rush," she says, grinning up at me.

I kiss her again. "That's right. No rush."

My phone interrupts the moment by buzzing in my pocket.

"Can you get that?" I ask Aurora.

She slides it out and hands it to me.

> Renn: Everyone to the back patio, please. We have ice cream melting.

*Oh shit.* "We have to go back."

"Me?"

"Yup, you, too."

She pulls her brows together, but I don't say anything more.

I start down the road with her still wrapped around me.

# Chapter Thirty

## Aurora

"Your family is *loud*," I say, laughing as Tate and I enter his house.

The air is perfumed with the scent of vanilla as if he's been burning the candles that suddenly filled a closet the other day. It was the same day as the fuzzy blankets appeared. A little suspicious but oh-so sweet.

Being back in his space fills me with a calmness that I now realize I'll never find anywhere else. I didn't have it in my own home. The Luxe, one of my favorite places, didn't deliver this sense of peace.

Or maybe it's a sense of home …

"They were extra loud because Renn brought rum," Tate says. "Did you see Bianca's husband's face?" He bursts out laughing. "I couldn't tell if he was disgusted by our behavior or amused by it."

"I think Foxx pretends to be a lot meaner than he is."

"You think?" Tate winces. "I don't know. You might be wrong

about this one. He used to be on my security detail, and he's one badass motherfucker."

"I didn't say he wasn't a badass motherfucker. I just said he scowls a lot, but I think it's a cover. Bet he's a softy."

Tate snorts. "I'd love for you to say that to his face."

"I'm not scared."

He takes my hands and leads me to the right, which is the opposite way from his bedroom.

"But I ..." I stop walking and point over my shoulder. "We're not going that way?"

"We have to talk first."

I groan, letting him pull me into the living room. "You talk too much."

He bursts out laughing.

"Tell me you have talking points so we can check them off as we go," I say, waiting for him to sit. As soon as his ass is on the cushion, I climb on top of him and straddle his lap. "Start talking."

His head leans back, his Adam's apple bobbing in his throat. "Aurora ..."

I place my hands on his shoulders.

"We have serious things to discuss," he says.

"You're the one who has the list, and you're not leading the conversation."

I start to wiggle against his erection, but his hands cinch my waist and keep me from moving.

"I was going to start with the potential of us having a baby, but now that you're sitting on my cock, we'll make that last," he says.

"Are you afraid you'll come in your pants again?"

He laughs. It's a warning. It's also so fucking hot.

"First, let's clarify this," he says. "We are in a monogamous, committed relationship. Right?"

I extend my arms and give him a look. "If you fuck anyone else, I swear to God, I'll go to prison."

He smirks, nodding his head. "Okay, but I do have a black lace bra upstairs. You can't get pissed if you find it."

Oh, I'm pissed.

"From who?" I ask, crossing my arms over my chest.

"This hottie I banged at a hotel the other night."

I start to climb off him, but he holds me down.

"She was so fucking sexy. I'm still obsessed with her tits."

"I fucking hate you."

He kisses me despite me trying to pull away. "Her name was Kelly."

I pull back and smack his chest. He finds this way too entertaining for how close he just came to death.

"What are our living arrangements going to be?" he asks.

"Pull that stunt again, and yours will be in a casket."

"Are we living apart? Together? Here? At your place? In a new place?"

"Oh, I don't know." I bite my lip. "My lease isn't up. So let's stay separate until then, and we can reassess."

"I'm adding this point in—"

"No! You can't lengthen the list of talking points," I say. "The only thing that is allowed to lengthen is right here."

Before he can react, I grind against him. I only get one whole movement in before he halts me.

"You are my girl," he says, peering into my eyes. "We're in a relationship. We might be having a baby. There's another thing we need to talk about in a second."

I lift a brow.

"But the point is, money is not an issue for you anymore," he says.

"No." I shake my head. "We can't talk money like this."

"Why?"

"It's weird. I'm not here for your money."

"I didn't say you were." He kisses the tip of my nose. "But having money is a part of my life. I can't ignore it. I must take precautions because of it. I don't walk around most places with a security detail, but I do have to be smart. You're going to have to be smart, too."

I shrug. "Fuck it. I'll just stay here as your sex slave. No security needed."

He laughs. "Well, that makes my next point obsolete."

"Good."

"I'm kidding." He reaches behind me onto the coffee table and pulls out a manila envelope. "This is for you."

My brows crinkle.

"Take it. Open it."

"Love mail day," I say, sarcasm thick in my voice. "Stop bouncing your legs. I'm going to slice my finger and get a paper cut."

"Just open the fucking thing."

My heartbeat quickens from his reaction. I'm not sure what's in this envelope, but it makes him nervous.

The possibilities are endless and terrifying, so I don't speculate.

"I started this a couple of weeks ago," he says. "This came through last night."

I pull out a packet of papers.

"Read the top one."

My chest heaves as I read the first few lines.

**FOR IMMEDIATE RELEASE**

**THE TENNESSEE RAPTORS** Announces Sale of **Franchise**

Nashville, Tennessee - The Tennessee Raptors announced today that the franchise will be sold to a new ownership group led by Tate Brewer and Aurora Johnson, pending final approval by the League's Board of Governors.

. . .

*The Situation*

Chills cover my skin as my gaze flips to Tate's. He's watching me warily.

"What ....What's this?" I ask with a half laugh. "I ... Is this a joke?"

I sit back and reread the papers. My mind is racing so fast that I can't compute anything it says.

"Gannon wanted out of Brewer Group, and none of us wants to take it over," he says softly. "We all had the option to buy out anything we wanted. And I thought buying the Raptors would be a great investment."

My jaw is sitting on my chest. "You realize I know nothing about managing a hockey team, right?"

"Me either." He laughs. "But we'll figure it out. This will also allow you to start from scratch. Put that plan you were telling me about together. See what you can do with it."

I grab his arm because I'm afraid I might fall over.

"You bought a franchise so I could see what I can do with it?" I ask, slowly blinking. "Tate, this is ... you might need to be committed."

"I needed the investment," he says easily. "This will allow you to control your space, your work, your life. You'll make a good salary, too. And this could be a good foundation for us to build on. We can't miss."

I throw myself against him, nestling my face in the crook of his neck. Tears pour down my cheeks as I'm overcome with emotion.

He pulls me tightly against him, rocking me back and forth. I can feel his love for me in his touch more than I can his actions. This man is the meaning of the word.

And he's also mine.

"I don't know what to say," I say, hiccuping a laugh. I pull back and wipe my eyes with my hands. "Does your family know you did this?"

"Yeah. We were going to announce it at the party. But we'd had an emotional twenty-four hours, and I didn't want to put you on the spot."

I cup his face in my hands. "Promise me something."

"Anything."

"What happened last night won't happen again. If we disagree, we'll figure it out before bed. No sleeping in this house unless we've worked through our shit."

He smirks. "Does this mean you're moving in?"

"Nope. I didn't say I was sleeping at my apartment. I just said I had a lease."

He laughs, his palms finding my ass.

"Thank you, Tate," I say, staring into his oceanic eyes. "Thank you for caring for me, believing in me, protecting me—*loving me.*" I grin. "And thank you for the Raptors. Can we change the name now?"

"It's yours." He shrugs. "Do whatever you want."

"Oh my God! That's why everything was halted lately!"

He nods as if I'm catching up. "There was no sense in wasting your time on something that wasn't going to see the light of day."

"What about Tally?"

"What about her?"

"Can we offer her my job? I mean, as the *owner of the franchise*, I assume I won't be answering vendor calls. Right?"

He shakes his head, amused. "You can literally do whatever you want. Hire. Fire. Move. Adjust. Change. Edit. Say no. Say yes. *It's yours, gorgeous.*"

"But what about you? It's yours, too."

"I'll be there to help if you need it. I'm hoping you'll give me a corner office across from yours."

"Done." I giggle. "This day has been mind-blowingly good. I owe you."

"On to point ... whatever number we're on," he says. "About this having a baby thing ..."

This time, he lets me move against him. "What about it?"

## The Situation

"Are you serious?"

"As a heart attack. I don't just want to be the hot stepmommy. I want to be the hot mommy, too."

He growls, gripping my hips and, this time, helps them move.

"I'm not getting any younger," I say, swiveling my hips. "And I want to be a mother while I still can. And I want to carry *your baby*."

"When?"

"I mean, we should start practicing now."

Tate leaps to his feet with me in his arms. My Raptors paperwork flutters to the floor.

"Hey!" I say, laughing. "Where are we going?"

"I can't have you sitting on my lap, grinding that little pussy all over me while talking about having my baby."

He captures my mouth with his, swallowing my moans.

Tate Brewer was only supposed to be a one-night stand. But being tossed on the bed while his lips travel south makes me realize that sometimes situations are meant to be.

And I wouldn't want it any other way.

### The End

If you've read the rest of the Brewer Family Series, make sure you don't miss **Bianca's book, FLAME**. It's available here.

Chapter One is next for your convenience.

Adriana Locke

*Flame Ebook Cover*

# Chapter One: FLAME

Foxx

"Are you having fun?" Banks slides next to me, a glass of lemonade in his hand. "That apple pie Honey made was the best pie I've ever had. Did you try it?"

I cock my head to the side and stare at him.

"Want me to get you a piece?" Banks asks, a wide smile plastered across his face.

I shift my weight from one foot to the other.

The air is filled with spices from the chili cook-off that took place an hour ago to benefit the local school's arts program. Conversations flow into a giant stream of noise as people catch up, recounting old high school sports games and current gossip.

*So much wasted energy.*

And in the midst of it all, my youngest brother is up to something. This isn't a revelation, nor is it a surprise. He's *always* up to something.

In the past few weeks, I've picked Banks up from jail in the

## Chapter One: FLAME

middle of the night. I watched him walk across the street covered in glitter—retribution for attaching stickers of his face to every surface of our brother Jess's house. One morning, I looked out the window to witness a giant metal rooster staring at me from across the road, thanks to Banks's handiwork and toddler-esque humor.

The guy is a menace but a predictable one. His tells are as clear as day, and right now, they're *screaming*.

"I've socialized enough," I say. "I'm heading home."

"*Already*? You just got here."

"I said I'd support the cause. I didn't say I'd stay all afternoon."

"But there's still so much to do. Did you even see my calendar? And I—"

"Why do you care what I do?" I cross my arms over my chest. I'm curious despite curiosity being against my better judgment. "I showed up. Yes, I saw your ridiculous calendar. I bought a pie. What more do you want from me?"

He points at me. "Can I have that pie, by the way? You snagged the last coconut cream."

"*No.*"

He holds up his hands. "Easy, tiger. I was kidding." He grimaces. "*Kind of*. Anyway, about you leaving ..."

I look at the ceiling and sigh.

This is precisely why I avoid human interaction as much as possible. I always walk away worse for the wear. I'm pushed too far or needled too much. Things are expected of me. My time and energy become commandeered, and I'm not into that sort of behavior.

It's not that I don't understand the concept behind group activities—I do. I took enough psychology classes to wrap my brain around it. People need to share their experiences and feel seen. The potential for success rises when people work together. Groups allow for high-level problem-solving and cooperation.

But me? I'd rather not be seen. I don't want to share my experiences. And I can damn well solve my own problems without someone like *Banks* weighing in.

## Chapter One: FLAME

"Are you listening to me?" Banks asks.

"No."

We turn our attention to the makeshift platform beside us. Gloria, an older woman Banks befriended in one of his silly schemes, taps a microphone. She beams from center stage.

"Ladies and gentlemen, please take your seats," she says, the microphone entirely too close to her teeth. She smiles at *me*. "It's time for the final event—the one you've all been waiting for. The bachelor auction is about to begin!"

My stomach knots at the look she's firing my way. *What's that all about? Does she think I'm Banks?*

He waves at her from beside me. She looks at him, then back at me, before returning her gaze to my brother.

*Yeah, Gloria. It's this goofy-ass guy you're after. Not me.*

Chatter breaks out through the room, and women scramble to find seats. Banks and I are nearly trampled as a group of ladies makes a beeline for the front row.

"Let's ... uh, move over here," Banks says, grabbing my elbow.

I flex my arm, and he promptly drops his hand, looking at me warily.

"Sorry," he says.

"Good life choice," I say.

"About that ..."

Banks sidesteps Marla, a silver-haired woman pushing her walker across the floor. Tennis balls cover the feet like drag slicks. Head down and shoulders back, she leans into the turn around the corner of the stage before nearly knocking over a small child to take the center seat.

"Have fun getting auctioned off," I say, turning to leave. "Looks like a good time."

"Foxx, *wait*."

The way he says my name, coupled with how he takes a half step back, has my instincts rippling with anticipation. *Something bad is about to happen.*

## Chapter One: FLAME

I square my shoulders with his. "What?"

He winces.

"I would like to welcome our four eligible bachelors on stage," Gloria says. "First, we have Shawn Daze, the surf instructor we all know and love. Welcome, Shawn!"

Cheers ring out from around the room as the first contestant takes his spot next to Gloria.

"Next, we have Chef Miguel Cotto, the reason we all go to La Pachanga," she says. "Welcome, Miguel!"

The applause grows louder.

Banks rocks back on his heels. "I need to tell you something."

"Colin Hensley, the firefighter that dreams are made of, is our third bachelor," Gloria says. "Say hello to our local hero!"

"Better hurry," I say. "You're next."

"About that ..."

"And, last, our final contestant. I don't know how we got this lucky, ladies," Gloria says. "Please welcome the one and only Foxx Carmichael!"

*What?*

Cheers fill the air. Everyone in the room fixes their gaze on me. Gloria watches me expectantly.

*Oh, hell no.*

Banks grimaces, moving even farther away from my right hand.

Everything inside me stills. My jaw flexes, and my teeth grind so hard they hurt.

"Tell me she got us mixed up," I say, balling my hands at my sides.

"Look, I can't be in the auction anymore. Sara will kill me. She's dangerous when she's mad."

"And I'm not?"

"Good point." His eyes dart around the room. "Listen, Foxx, I didn't think about it until we arrived. I can't let my girl Gloria down, and none of our brothers can fill in. Maddox has Ashley, Moss has Brooke. Pippa would murder Jess if I volunteered him."

## Chapter One: FLAME

"Foxx? Can you join us on stage, please?" Gloria asks, the microphone squealing in her hand. She taps on it, making it even worse. "Can someone show me how to adjust this thing?"

The entire town stares holes in my back, waiting for me to take the trail of humiliation and occupy the spot by Colin. Hushed conversations whisper through the room. I'm sure jokes are being made over coffee and coffee cake.

*"Please do this for me,"* Banks says, holding his hands before him. "I panicked, Foxx. I didn't know what to do. You are the only one of us who's single, and I ... *I panicked, Foxx.*"

"You're repeating yourself."

"It's for a good cause, and it's not like you have a bursting social calendar."

"Foxx?" Gloria asks again.

Banks grins. "You're drawing more attention to yourself by not going up there, you know."

I take a step toward him. "Sleep with one eye open, you little fucker."

Instead of looking worried, he manages to look relieved.

I don't really have a choice because, for once in his damn life, Banks is right. I'm only creating a bigger problem by resisting. The chatter among the gossips will only worsen if I duck out the back door and leave them hanging.

*Banks, you're living on borrowed time, kid.*

I straighten my shirt, stand tall, and take a long, deep breath. *Focus on revenge. It will be so, so sweet.*

I step purposely onto the stage, carefully avoiding eye contact with the audience. My heart races as I stand next to the firefighter. He gives me a slight nod, a gesture of pity, really, before turning his attention back to the women clutching paddles with numbers written in black magic marker.

Gloria drones on and on, thanking everyone who had the tiniest hand in putting the event together. Then she gives a quick rendition

## Chapter One: FLAME

of the rules. While she reads the bullet points off a sheet of paper, I exhale and finally face the crowd.

The women in my family sit at a round table near the bathroom. My mother is more entertained than she should be. Dad stands next to Jess, the only brother I really like most days, and lifts a plastic cup my way. My failure to acknowledge him results in a chuckle that he's lucky I can't hear. Banks stands next to Jess and gives me a thumbs-up. I level my gaze with his, unblinking.

His smile slowly fades, and his thumb falls from the air like a deflated balloon. I enjoy a smidgen of satisfaction from that.

"Let's start the bidding on Shawn at two hundred dollars," Gloria says. "Do I have any takers?"

Paddles are thrust into the air. It's one of the most embarrassing things I've ever witnessed.

*Could I just donate a large sum of money and spare us all the trouble?*

Sweat dots the nape of my neck as the bids for Shawn increase.

"One thousand dollars for Shawn! Going once, going twice—a date with Shawn is sold to Mrs. Ferguson," Gloria says, pointing at a petite older lady with a purse embroidered with cats. "Congratulations!"

*Fuck my life.*

*And fuck Banks's life since we're at it.*

I turn to Gloria, lips parted to announce my benevolent donation, but the wind is knocked out of me.

*What is she doing here?*

Bianca Brewer stands in the entryway, chatting with a woman holding a long roll of raffle tickets like they're long-lost friends. Except they're not. Bianca has never been to Kismet Beach before.

"On to Miguel," Gloria says. "Since the last bachelor raised so much money, let's start a bit higher this time. Do I have five hundred?"

My body catches fire as Bianca moves across the room.

Landry Security assigned me to her security detail three years

## Chapter One: FLAME

ago. Despite having a binder of information before meeting her, nothing could have prepared me for the powerhouse of Bianca Elaine Brewer.

She's five foot five with shoulder-length auburn hair. Her eyes are pieces of jade that can see right through you. She has high cheekbones, deep curves, and a cute button nose.

*She fascinates me.*

The woman is wildly intelligent. Watching her bring a boardroom of men to their knees is one of the hottest things I've ever seen. She's curious and confident yet humble and kind. And she doesn't give a damn about what she should and shouldn't do. She does what she wants.

Unfortunately, that can't be me.

Bianca looks up. Her green eyes shine when they connect with mine.

*Shit.*

"Hey," she says, mouthing the word from across the room.

I struggle to remain unaffected, but the corners of my lips lift. She notices. She always finds the chink in my armor. A smile creeps over her pink pout, hitting me directly in the cock.

*Get yourself together, Carmichael.*

"Going once, going twice—a date with Miguel is sold to Mrs. Daniels for twelve hundred dollars!" Gloria announces.

My brows pull together as Jason, Bianca's brother and my best friend—my only friend—enters the building. His solemn expression is replaced with amusement as he realizes what he's about to witness.

I flash him a pointed look to watch himself. It only makes him laugh.

*Maybe I don't like him either.*

"Next up is Colin," Gloria says. "Let's start the bidding at five hundred. Do I see six?"

Jason and Bianca take a seat in the back row. He folds his hands on his lap like he's settling in for a show. She takes a bid paddle from the raffle ticket lady.

## Chapter One: FLAME

This is the nail in Banksy's coffin.

"I have six," Gloria says. "Do I see seven?"

Bianca's eyes find mine again.

"There's seven. Do I have eight?" Gloria asks.

Bianca lifts a brow, pressing her lips together.

*What does that mean? Do you want a date with Colin?*

As if she reads my mind, she raises her paddle.

I raise a brow back.

"There's eight. Do I have nine?" Gloria asks the room.

Bianca shrugs innocently, daring me to react. But I don't. And I won't.

She might get under my skin like no one I've met before, but I refuse to cross that line.

I was the lead on her security detail for two and a half years, and for two and a half years the woman whittled away at my restraint. It's impossible to resist her. Her little smile and the way her nose wrinkles when she's being cheeky. Her penchant for burgers and vanilla shakes. Her perfume and her ability to wear a T-shirt and cocktail dress with the same understated elegance.

*The way she says my name.*

Our relationship shifted over time. It began strictly professionally before transitioning to more of a friendship. And then, during the past six months, we were toeing a line that shouldn't be crossed.

Conversations weren't strictly business. Smiles were exchanged when no one was looking. Our touches lingered long after contact should've been broken.

I wasn't thinking of her as my boss. I was thinking about her bent over her desk. I was imagining her in my bed wearing my T-shirt. I had visions of her in my truck, her hand in mine, doing mundane tasks like running errands.

But it was harmless. It was simply a war inside me that I was winning.

And then one night changed everything. That's the night six

## Chapter One: FLAME

months ago that I asked for an immediate transfer ... and I haven't seen her privately since.

"Sold! A date with Colin to Mrs. Breckenridge for one thousand one hundred dollars." Gloria peeks around the others and smiles at me. "I'm starting the bid on our final bachelor with a bid of my own at five hundred dollars. Do I have six hundred for Foxx?"

All eyes land on me. I'm not sure where to look. I don't want to see my family laughing; I want to like them tomorrow. I can't look at Banks because I'll be tempted to leap off the stage and beat his ass right here. I don't want to look at anyone bidding, lest they think I want them to spend their hard-earned dollars on a date with me. And I sure as hell don't want to make eye contact with Bianca.

"Six hundred from Marla in the front," Gloria says. "Do I have seven?"

Various paddles shoot to the ceiling. *And they stay there.*

Gloria laughs. "I see. Let's go to eight hundred?" The paddles remain in the air. "Nine? One thousand? One thousand one hundred?"

*What the hell is happening?*

"Fifteen hundred!" Marla grabs her walker to brace herself. "I bid fifteen hundred."

"Okay. Sixteen hundred, anyone?" Gloria asks. "Yes! I have sixteen hundred from the lady in the back."

Heads turn to the back of the room. Bianca sits tall in her seat, proudly waving her paddle.

I look at Jason in surprise. He shrugs as if there's nothing he can do. I send him a silent message to stop her. But instead of intervening like I've seen him do countless times in both private and combat situations, he defers.

He's helpless and at the mercy of his baby sister.

"Seventeen hundred!" Marla shouts, her voice wavering from the force of her words.

"Eighteen hundred," Bianca fires back.

## Chapter One: FLAME

"Two thousand," Marla says, her hands shaking. She narrows her eyes at Bianca.

Out of my periphery, I notice Banks snickering.

"Two thousand, two hundred." Bianca's voice is edgier than before as she stares Marla down. "I bid two thousand, two hundred dollars."

Jason gets up and stands behind her, holding his forehead.

"Two thousand, three hundred," Marla says.

"Twenty-five hundred."

Heads swing from one side of the room to the other as bids volley back and forth.

Marla scoots her walker around so she's face-to-face with Bianca. "Twenty-seven hundred."

"Twenty-eight," Bianca says easily.

Marla's finger shakes as she points at her adversary. "Respect your elders, missy!" Her gaze whips to Gloria. "*Three thousand.*"

"Someone stop this," I mumble.

Bianca stands, holding her paddle in the air, and levels her gaze at Marla. "Ten thousand dollars."

*What did she just say?*

Gasps echo through the room.

"I'm sorry, hon," Gloria says, the microphone squealing. "Did you just bid *ten thousand dollars?*"

Bianca smiles sheepishly. "It's for charity, right?"

Marla flops in her chair, defeated.

Applause breaks out as Gloria struggles through her shock, her gaze switching between Bianca and me. I feel like Gloria expects me to say something, but I have nothing to say other than *what the fuck just happened?*

My head spins.

I exit the stage, ignoring curious looks from the audience as everyone gets up to leave.

I came for pie.

*Pie.*

*Chapter One: FLAME*

*What went so wrong?*

My feet falter, and I stop just short of where my brother and I stood only minutes ago.

*Banks.*

*Banks is what went wrong.*

I growl into the air.

*Today can't possibly get any worse.*

But, does it get worse? Find out by clicking here.

# Acknowledgments

I have so many people to thank for helping get The Situation to print. But let me start off by thanking my Creator—for everything.

My family is my great source of joy and inspiration. A big thank you to my husband, four boys, and bonus parents for always being in my corner and showering me with patience and love. You're the best cheerleaders ever and I couldn't possibly love you all more.

I am so, so very blessed to have a fantastic team of brilliant, powerful, and kind women in my life: Mandi Beck (the author of Love Hurts, the book from Gannon's bookshelf and my very best friend), S.L. Scott (I can't start my day without coffee and our chats), Jessica Prince (we don't have to hike the whole Appalachian trail!), Anjelica Grace, Kenna Rey, and Carina Rose (my Italian expert).

I would also like to thank Kari March for an incredible model cover, Michelle Lancaster for the stunning photo, and Books and Moods for the perfect special edition cover. Your talents wow me!

Also, I couldn't have created this story without Marion Archer (Marion Making Manuscripts) and Jenny Sims (Editing 4 Indies). I love you both so much. Thank you for your incredible patience and friendship.

There are also so many women behind the scenes who keep the Locke World running, including Tiffany Remy, Jennifer Hess, Kaitie Reister, Stephanie Gibson, Jordan Fazzini, and Sue Maturo. You're the best team ever. Also a huge shoutout to the team at Valentine PR. Thank you all for all you do!

Finally, to my readers—you are the greatest thing to ever happen to me (aside from my family). You stick by me and cheer me on no matter what. I can't explain how much that means to me. I love each and every one of you.

Xo, Addy ♥

# About the Author

USA Today Bestselling author, Adriana Locke, writes contemporary romances about the two things she knows best—big families and small towns. Her stories are about ordinary people finding extraordinary love with the perfect combination of heart, heat, and humor.

She loves connecting with readers, fall weather, football, reading alpha heroes, everything pumpkin, and pretending to garden.

Hailing from a tiny town in the Midwest, Adriana spends her free time with her high school sweetheart (who she married over twenty years ago) and their four sons (who truly are her best work).

Her kitchen may be a perpetual disaster, and if all else fails, there is always pizza.

Join her reader group and talk all the bookish things by clicking here.

www.adrianalocke.com

Made in United States
Orlando, FL
26 May 2025